Cookie Exchange

Third in the Colorado Collection Series

Written and Compiled by
CYNDI DUNCAN and GEORGIE PATRICK

Illustrated by
COLETTE B. McLAUGHLIN

D0967567

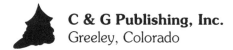

C & G Publishing, Inc.
Greeley, Colorado

Cookie Exchange

Published by:

C&G Publishing, Inc.
P.O. Box 5199
Greeley, CO 80634-0103
1-800-925-3172

DEDICATION

We dedicate this book to the memory of our friend Rosi, who enthusiastically attended each cookie exchange. We miss you, Rosi.

ACKNOWLEDGEMENTS

We appreciate the contributions to <u>Cookie Exchange</u> made by our friends and families.

Thanks to those friends who attended our cookie exchanges:

Cheryl Adams	Eileen Huff
Rosi Anson	Pat James
Mary Aschenbrenner	Jan Jerome
Donna Behning	Bobbi Kiser
Pat Best	Bonnie Lindstrom
Cheryl Brewster	Barb Lowenbach
Lynn Byers	Irene Lowenbach
Joanie Carvajal	Patty Marriner
Lara Clark	Tresa Martinez
Dona Cooper	Colette McLaughlin
Eileen Croissant	Becky Modlin
Sharol Darling	Sue Nicholas
Sue Elton	Libby Oliver
Gretchen Ensz	Valerie Olson
Marilyn Everett	Kathy Painter
Pat Fay	Dee Powers
Carol Feit	Pam Reynolds
Zona Felderman	Sara Roy
Sarah Fink	Ann Schrader
Reda Foard	Jean Schreck
Carolyn Forkner	Sue Simmons
Dixie Fraser	Salley Smith
Kathy Freese	Gudi Spurlin
Verneine Gebbie	Sheryl Steel
Linda Hannan	Pat Thomas
Bert Hays	Fern Tice
Carol Heinze	Ruth Vaas
Sandy Helgeson	JoLynn Winger
Kappy Hesse	Fran Wood

Thanks to these contributors:

Vicki Croot	Jerry Minerich
Valerie DiBenedetto	Lucille Morrison
Barb Hendricks	Karin Oeffling
Nancy Kagan	Tracey Randel
Sharon Lunbeck	Betty Schenk
	Barb Smith

A special thanks to Heather, Shawn, Wendi, Toni, Wade, Heidi, Bob and L.G. for all their love and support.

INTRODUCTION

Cookie Exchange, the name says it all. We have continued to collect cookie recipes from the Christmas cookie exchanges we've hosted and have added a few of our favorites as well. Cookie Exchange is a delightful blend of our bestselling Colorado Cookie Collection and the award winning design of our Nothin' but Muffins. In addition, we have responded to your requests for low fat cookie recipes and have added a section just for you.

Cookie Exchange offers the best in cookie recipes, not only for the holidays, but for all year round - whether you cook at sea level or in high-altitude kitchens. Our recipes are written in an easy-to-follow format and are double indexed for your convenience. The handy wire binding helps make baking easy, and the beautiful cover design enhances any kitchen decor. After fifteen years, demands from our publishing business dictate that we entertain our friends at a time far removed from the holidays. So, we held our fifteenth and final cookie exchange in December of 1993. We consider ourselves fortunate to have so many good friends. We will always appreciate them and make time for new ones.

Cookie Exchange contains recipes from those friends who attended our exchanges during the last five years. On the following page are suggestions for hosting your own cookie exchange. Have fun!!

HOST YOUR OWN COOKIE EXCHANGE

Like any new venture, the first time out is a real learning experience. Our first cookie exchange was no exception. We found that in order to make our exchange successful we needed a "little" structure, a lot of laughter, good friends and a bottle of wine to celebrate our success. Here is our step-by-step guide to a successful cookie exchange; don't forget to add the special touches that make it yours.

Step 1: Plan
- •Organize date and guest list
- •Decide on invitation format including when recipes are due, how many cookies to bring, and how they should be packaged.
- •Plan for the cookie exchange day.

Step 2: Preparation
- •Gather supplies (door prizes, napkins, plates, coffee, tea, cups, decorations, pop flats for taking cookies home, tissue paper, bell, tables).
- •Make name tags.
- •Make 2 place cards per cookie recipe (one for tasting table and one for exchange table).
- •Type, print and put together recipe booklets (the tree we always used as our cover later became the cover of our first book, Colorado Cookie Collection and the logo for C & G Publishing, Inc.).
- •Arrange for helpers if the guest list is large (our largest turn out was 72 guests).
- •Make your own cookies (if possible make your recipe ahead of time and freeze, if not block out time the day before the exchange).

Step 3: Clean and decorate your house
   (great motivation for early holiday decorating).

Step 4: The big day
1. Set up drinks area (don't forget to make the coffee).
2. Pin name tags on booklets and arrange alphabetically.
3. Put door prizes and bell in convenient location.
4. Arrange place cards on tasting and exchange tables.
5. Set plate at each place on the tasting table.
6. Instruct helpers (monitor exchange tables).
7. Enjoy your friends, celebrate your success and clean up.

Bar
Cookies

BAR COOKIES INDEX

PUMPKIN-DATE BARS

1 cup all-purpose flour
3/4 cup sugar
1 teaspoon baking powder
1 teaspoon ground cinnamon
1/2 teaspoon baking soda
1/8 teaspoon ground cloves
1/8 teaspoon salt
1 cup canned pumpkin
1/2 cup vegetable oil
2 eggs, beaten
3/4 cup dates, chopped or snipped
1/2 cup chopped walnuts
Powdered sugar

Combine flour, sugar, baking powder, cinnamon, soda, cloves, and salt in a medium bowl. Stir in pumpkin, oil and eggs until thoroughly combined. Stir in dates and walnuts.
   Spread the batter into an ungreased 13x9x2-inch baking pan. Bake in a 350° oven about 15 minutes or until a wooden toothpick inserted near the center comes out clean. Cool in pan on wire rack. Sift powdered sugar over top. Cut into bars. Makes 30.

CHEWY SCOTCH SQUARES

1 cube margarine
1 cup brown sugar
1/3 cup preserves (peach or apricot)
3/4 cup flour
1 teaspoon baking powder
1/2 teaspoon salt
1 1/2 cups oatmeal

Mix margarine, sugar and preserves together. Add remaining ingredients. Spread mixture to within one-inch of edge of a greased 13x9-inch pan. Bake at 325° for 25 minutes. Cool and cut into squares.

PECAN DIAMONDS

1 cup unsifted all-purpose flour
1/2 cup granulated sugar
1/2 cup brown sugar
1 cup unsalted butter
2 tablespoons honey
2 cups pecan halves
1 tablespoon heavy cream

Preheat oven to 375°. Grease 9-inch pan; line with foil. In bowl, mix flour and granulated sugar. With pastry blender or fork, cut in 1/2 cup butter until mixture resembles coarse crumbs; with floured fingers, press in pan. Bake 10 minutes.

In saucepan, heat remaining butter, brown sugar and honey until melted and bubbly. Add nuts and cream; pour over crust; bake 20 minutes or until bubbly. Cool in pan. Lift cookie from pan; remove foil. Cut cookie into 8 strips; cut into diamond shapes. Makes about 5 dozen cookies.

GERMAN CHOCOLATE DESSERT BARS

1 package German Chocolate cake mix
1 1/2 cups quick oats
1/2 cup butter, softened
1 can coconut pecan or coconut almond frosting
8-ounce package cream cheese, softened
3 eggs

Heat oven to 350°. Grease 13x9-inch pan. In large bowl, combine cake mix, oats, butter and 1 egg. Mix until crumbly. Reserve 2 cups crumb mixture for topping. Press remaining crumb mixture into bottom of prepared pan.

In same large bowl, blend frosting, cream cheese and 2 eggs. Beat at high speed for one minute. Pour over crust. Sprinkle with reserved crumbs. Bake at 350° (375° for high altitudes) for 45-55 minutes. Cut into bars. Store in refrigerator. Makes 36 bars.

CARAMEL OATMEAL BARS

1 1/2 cups flour
1 1/2 cups oatmeal
1 cup brown sugar
3/4 teaspoon soda
1/4 teaspoon salt
1 cup plus 2 tablespoons butter or margarine, melted
1 cup chocolate chips
1/2 cup nuts
3/4 cup caramel topping
3 tablespoons flour

Mix dry ingredients. Add margarine. Reserve half of mixture. Pat remaining half of mixture into 9x9-inch pan. Bake at 350° 10 minutes.

Sprinkle chocolate chips and nuts on top of crust. Combine caramel and flour and drizzle over chips and nuts. Crumble remaining crust over tops and press lightly. Bake at 350° for 15-20 minutes. Cool before cutting into squares.

ALMOND TOFFEE

1 cube butter
1 cube margarine
1/2 cup plus 2 tablespoons sugar
1 package club crackers
1 cup sliced almonds

Foil line 18x12-inch jelly roll cookie sheet and spray foil with cooking spray. Spread 1 package club crackers on pan. Sprinkle almonds on crackers. Boil first 3 ingredients for 1 minute. Pour boiled mixture on crackers. Bake 10 minutes at 350°. Cut apart with pizza cutter before cooling.

3

CHOCOLATE CHIP BRICKLE BARS

1/2 cup margarine
1 1/2 cups graham cracker crumbs
1 14-ounce can sweetened condensed milk
1 6-ounce package almond brickle chips
1 6-ounce package semisweet chocolate chips
1 cup nuts, chopped

Preheat oven to 350°. Melt margarine and combine with graham cracker crumbs. Spread in 13x9-inch baking pan. Pour sweetened condensed milk evenly over crumbs. Top with remaining ingredients in order listed. Press down firmly. Bake at 350° for 20-25 minutes or until lightly browned. Cool. Chill, if desired. Cut into bars. Store covered at room temperature.

MOUND BARS

1/2 cup butter
2 cups graham cracker crumbs
1/2 cup powdered sugar

Combine and pat in13x9-inch or 2 8x8-inch pans. Bake at 350° for 10 minutes.

Filling:

1 can sweetened condensed milk
2 cups flaked coconut
1 teaspoon vanilla

Combine and spread on crust. Bake at 350° for 10 minutes. Remove from oven and immediately lay 10 chocolate almond bars on crust layer. Spread when melted.

CHERRY WALNUT BARS

2 1/4 cups flour
1/2 cup sugar
1 cup margarine or butter, softened
2 eggs
1 cup brown sugar
1/2 teaspoon salt
1/2 teaspoon baking powder
1/2 teaspoon vanilla
1 teaspoon butter flavoring
1/2 cup maraschino cherries, chopped (reserve juice)
1/2 cup walnuts, chopped
1/2 cup coconut

Mix together flour, 1/2 cup sugar and margarine. Press into a 13x9-inch pan. Bake for 20 minutes at 350°.
Blend remaining ingredients together and pour over crust (it is okay if it is still warm). Bake for an additional 25 minutes. Cool well and frost.

Frosting:

2 tablespoons butter or margarine
2 cups powdered sugar
Cherry juice, enough to produce a spreadable frosting

Mix together and frost. Cut into 1 inch squares.

EASY FOUR LAYER MARSHMALLOW BARS

1 package (2 layer size) chocolate or yellow cake mix
1/4 cup margarine, melted
1/4 cup water
3 cups miniature marshmallows
1 cup multi-colored milk chocolate candies
1/2 cup peanuts, chopped

Heat oven to 375°. Mix cake mix, margarine and water until blended. Pat into greased 13x9-inch baking pan. Bake for 20-22 minutes. Remove and layer marshmallows, candies and peanuts over crust. Bake 2-3 minutes or until marshmallows begin to melt. Cool. Cut into bars. Makes 24 bars.

Variation: Substitute 1 cup chocolate chips, 1/2 cup coconut and 1/2 cup chopped pecans for multi-colored candies and peanuts.

SALTED PEANUT BARS

3 cups flour
1 cup margarine
1 1/2 cups brown sugar
1/4 teaspoon salt
2 6-ounce packages butterscotch chips
1/2 cup white corn syrup
3 tablespoons water
3 tablespoons margarine
2/3 cups salted peanuts

Mix flour, margarine, sugar and salt together. Pat in jelly roll pan. Bake 10 minutes at 375°

Combine chips, corn syrup, water and margarine in double boiler and heat until melted. Add peanuts and spread over baked crust as soon as taken from oven. Return to oven for 8 minutes at 350°. Cool and cut into bars.

TOFFEE BARS

1 cup butter or margarine
1 cup brown sugar
1 teaspoon vanilla
2 cups enriched flour, sifted
1 6-ounce package semisweet chocolate pieces
1 cup walnuts, chopped

Thoroughly cream together butter, sugar and vanilla. Add flour; mix well. Stir in chocolate and walnuts. Press mixture into ungreased 15 1/2x10 1/2x1-inch jelly roll pan. Bake at 350° for 25 minutes or until browned. While warm, cut into bars or squares. Cool before removing from pan. Makes about 5 dozen bars.

CRANBERRY BARS

1 1/2 cups flour
1 1/2 cups oats
3/4 cup brown sugar, packed
1 teaspoon lemon peel, shredded
1/4 teaspoon baking soda
1/4 cup margarine, melted
1 16-ounce can whole cranberry sauce
1/4 cup pecans, chopped

In a large bowl, combine flour, oats, brown sugar, lemon peel and soda. Add margarine and mix thoroughly. Reserve 1 cup mixture for topping. Pat remaining mixture into ungreased 12x7 1/2x2-inch pan. Bake at 350° for 20 minutes. Carefully spread cranberry sauce over baked crust. Stir nuts into remaining oat mixture. Sprinkle over cranberry layer. Lightly pat oat mixture into sauce. Bake at 350° for 25-30 minutes longer until top is golden. Cool on wire rack and cut into bars.

NUTTY MARSHMALLOW BARS

1 cup salted blanched peanuts, chopped
3/4 cup all-purpose flour
3/4 cup quick-cooking or regular oats
2/3 cup packed brown sugar
1/2 teaspoon baking soda
1/2 teaspoon salt
1 egg
1/3 cup margarine or butter, softened
1 jar (7 ounces) marshmallow creme
1/3 cup caramel ice-cream topping
1 cup salted blanched peanuts

Heat oven to 350°. Stir chopped peanuts, flour, oats, brown sugar, baking soda, salt and egg in large bowl. Stir in margarine until mixture is crumbly.

Press in ungreased rectangular pan, 13x9x2 inches. Bake 10 minutes. Spoon marshmallow creme over hot layer. Let stand 1 minute; spread evenly. Drizzle topping over creme; sprinkle with 1 cup peanuts.

Bake until golden brown, about 20 minutes. Let stand until cool, then loosen edges from side of pan with wet knife. Cut into 1 1/2-inch bars with wet knife. Makes 24 bars.

MISSISSIPPI MUD BARS

4 eggs
1 cup butter or margarine, softened
2 cups sugar
1 teaspoon vanilla extract
1 1/2 cups all-purpose flour
1/4 cup unsweetened cocoa
Dash salt
1 cup pecans, chopped
1 7-ounce jar marshmallow creme

Preheat oven to 350°. Grease a 13x9-inch baking pan; set aside. In large mixing bowl with mixer at medium speed, beat eggs, butter or margarine, sugar and vanilla until light and fluffy, scraping sides of bowl occasionally. Add flour, cocoa and salt; beat just until well blended. Fold in pecans. Spread batter evenly in pan. Bake 40 to 45 minutes. Immediately place dollops of marshmallow creme on cake; spread until smooth. Let cool on wire rack for at least 1 hour before frosting (or chill until set, about 30 minutes).

Frosting:

1/3 cup butter or margarine
1/2 cup unsweetened cocoa
1/3 cup milk
1 tsp. vanilla extract
2 1/2 cups powdered sugar

In medium saucepan melt butter or margarine; stir in cocoa and cook 1 minute. Remove from heat. Add remaining frosting ingredients, stir until smooth. Spread on top of marshmallow creme. When frosting has cooled, cut into 1-inch squares. Makes 7 dozen bars.

YULETIDE TOFFEE SQUARES

4 1/2 cups oats
1 cup brown sugar
3/4 cup margarine, softened
1/2 cup corn syrup
1 tablespoon vanilla
1/2 teaspoon salt
1 12-ounce package chocolate chips
2/3 cup nuts, chopped

Combine oats, brown sugar, margarine, corn syrup, vanilla and salt. Mix well and firmly press mixture into greased 15x10-inch jelly roll pan. Bake at 400° for 18 minutes. Immediately sprinkle chocolate chips evenly over toffee. Let stand 10 minutes. Spread chocolate evenly over toffee and sprinkle with nuts. Cool and cut into squares.

JACKPOT BARS

1 box yellow cake mix
1/4 cup margarine, melted
1 egg
3 cups miniature marshmallows
1 stick margarine
1 12-ounce package peanut butter chips
1/2 cup corn syrup
1 teaspoon vanilla
2 cups Spanish peanuts
2 cups rice krispies

Combine cake mix, melted margarine and egg. Press into a 13x9-inch pan. Bake 10 minutes at 350°. Place marshmallows on top and return to oven for about 3 minutes until marshmallows puff up. Melt chips, syrup and butter. Add vanilla. Pour over peanuts and rice krispies. Spread over marshmallows. Refrigerate until cool. Cut into bars.

PECAN PIE BARS

1 2-layer size yellow cake mix
1/4 cup margarine or butter, softened
1 egg, beaten

Set aside 2/3 cup of the yellow cake mix. Combine remaining
cake mix, margarine or butter and beaten egg. Stir by hand
until mixture is crumbly. Press evenly over bottom and one
inch up the sides of an ungreased 13x9x2-inch baking pan.
Bake in 350° oven for 15 minutes.

Filling:

3 eggs
1 cup light corn syrup
1/2 cup brown sugar, packed
1 teaspoon vanilla
1 cup pecans, chopped

Combine first four ingredients. Add reserved cake mix. Stir
mixture by hand until thoroughly combined. Spread filling
evenly over the baked crust and sprinkle with chopped pecans.
Bake at 350° for 30-35 minutes or until filling is set. Cool
completely. Cut into 32 bars.

TRIPLE LAYER CHOCOLATE BARS

1 1/2 cups graham cracker crumbs
1/2 cup cocoa
1/4 cup sugar
1/2 cup margarine or butter, melted
1 14-ounce can sweetened condensed milk (NOT
    evaporated milk)
1/4 cup flour
1 egg
1 teaspoon vanilla
1/2 teaspoon baking powder
3/4 cup nuts, chopped
1 12-ounce package semisweet chocolate chips

Preheat oven to 350°. Combine crumbs, 1/4 cup cocoa, sugar and butter or margarine; press firmly on bottom of 13x9-inch baking pan. In mixing bowl, beat 1/4 cup cocoa, sweetened condensed milk, flour, egg, vanilla and baking powder together. Stir in nuts and chips. Spread over prepared crust. Top with chips. Bake 20-25 minutes or until set. Cool. Cut into 24-36 bars. Store tightly covered at room temperature.

CARAMEL PECAN DREAM BARS

1 yellow cake mix
1/3 cup margarine, softened
1 egg
1 14-ounce can sweetened condensed milk
1 teaspoon vanilla
1 cup pecans, chopped
1 cup chocolate-covered brickle candy pieces

Combine cake mix, margarine and egg. Pat into a 13x9-inch pan. Stir together remaining ingredients and spread over mixture in pan. Bake at 350° for 25-35 minutes. Center will appear loose but sets up with cooling. Cut into 24 bars.

CHEWY GOOEY GOOBER BARS

1 20-ounce package refrigerated chocolate chip cookie
    dough
1 cup salted peanuts, chopped
1 1/2 cups mini marshmallows
1/2 cup peanut butter chips
1/2 cup semisweet chocolate chips
1/2 cup caramel ice cream topping

Heat oven to 350°. Slice cookie dough as directed on package. Arrange slices in bottom of ungreased 15x10x1-inch baking pan. Using floured fingers press dough evenly into pan. Bake at 350° for 8-10 minutes. Sprinkle crust with peanuts, chips and marshmallows. Bake another 10-12 minutes, or until marshmallows are light golden brown. Remove form oven. Drizzle caramel topping evenly over bars. Cool completely. Makes 32 bars.

COCONUT CHEWS

3/4 cup shortening (half butter or margarine), softened
3/4 cup powdered sugar
1 1/2 cups all-purpose flour
2 eggs
1 cup brown sugar, packed
2 tablespoons flour
1/2 teaspoon baking powder
1/2 teaspoon salt
1/2 teaspoon vanilla
1/2 cup walnuts, chopped
1/2 cup flaked coconut

Heat oven to 350°. Cream shortening and powdered sugar. Blend in 1 1/2 cups flour. Press evenly in bottom of ungreased 13x9x2-inch baking pan. Bake 12-15 minutes. Mix remaining ingredients; spread over hot baked layer and bake 20 minutes longer. While warm, spread with icing. Cool. Cut into bars. Makes 32 cookies.

Orange-lemon Icing:

1 1/2 cups powdered sugar
2 tablespoons butter or margarine, melted
3 tablespoons orange juice
3 teaspoons lemon juice

Mix until smooth and of spreading consistency.

CHOCOLATE MINT BROWNIES

1/2 cup butter or margarine, softened
3/4 cup sugar
1 cup all-purpose flour
1/3 cup cocoa
1/4 cup dark corn syrup
1/2 teaspoon baking powder
1/4 teaspoon salt
2 eggs
1 6-ounce package semisweet chocolate pieces
3/4 cup walnuts, coarsely chopped
1 6-ounce box chocolate-coated peppermint cream
      wafers (about 25 one-inch squares)
1/2 cup powdered sugar
2 teaspoons water

Preheat oven to 350°. Grease 9x9-inch baking pan.
    In a small bowl with mixer at high speed, beat butter or margarine and sugar until light and fluffy. Reduce speed to low; add flour, cocoa, corn syrup, baking powder, salt and eggs. Beat ingredients until well mixed, occasionally scraping bowl with rubber spatula. Stir in semisweet chocolate pieces and walnuts. Spread batter evenly into prepared pan. Bake 20 minutes. Remove pan from oven; evenly arrange mint wafers on top of baked layer. Return pan to oven. Bake 10 minutes longer. Cool brownies on a wire rack.
    In small bowl, mix powdered sugar and water until icing is smooth. Drizzle icing over brownies. Cut into 25 squares. Cover and refrigerate up to three days.

SCANDINAVIAN ALMOND BARS

1 3/4 cups all-purpose flour
2 teaspoons baking powder
1/4 teaspoon salt
1/2 cup butter or margarine
1 cup sugar
1 egg
1/2 teaspoon almond extract
Milk
1/2 cup sliced almonds, coarsely chopped
Almond icing

Stir together flour, baking powder and salt. In large mixing bowl beat butter or margarine until softened. Add sugar, egg and almond extract; beat until well mixed. Divide dough into fourths. Form each into a 12-inch roll. Place two rolls 4 to 5 inches apart on an ungreased cookie sheet. Flatten to 3-inches wide. Repeat with remaining rolls. Brush flattened rolls with milk and sprinkle with almonds. Bake in a 325° oven for 12-14 minutes or until edges are lightly browned. While cookies are still warm, cut them crosswise at a diagonal into 1-inch strips. Cool. Drizzle with Almond Icing.

Almond Icing:

1 cup powdered sugar, sifted
1/4 teaspoon almond extract
Enough milk (3-4 teaspoons) to make icing of drizzling
    consistency

Beat together until smooth and drizzle over bars.

HINT: While bar cookies are still warm and soft on the cookie sheet, use a sharp knife to cut the baked dough diagonally into one-inch strips. Cool the strips on a wire rack before drizzling with icing.

PEANUT BUTTER SHORTBREAD BARS

2 cups plus 2 tablespoons all-purpose flour
1/2 cup sugar
2 tablespoons cornstarch
1/2 cup cold butter
1 cup crunchy or smooth peanut butter, divided in half
2/3 cup powdered sugar
3 tablespoons milk
1/2 cup pecans or peanuts, chopped
1/2 cup of your choice of: semi-sweet chocolate chips,
     chopped candy-coated chocolate candies,
     chopped chocolate-covered toffee candy, butter-
     scotch chips, etc.

Combine flour, sugar and cornstarch in medium bowl. Using pastry blender, cut in the butter and 1/2 cup peanut butter until the mixture resembles coarse crumbs. (Mixture will be dry.) Press mixture into a 9x9-inch baking pan. Bake at 350° for 40 minutes. Let cool. Mix powdered sugar, remaining 1/2 cup peanut butter and milk, until blended. Spread on top of shortbread. Sprinkle top with nuts and choice of crushed toppings, pressing lightly. Allow to set briefly. Cut into 2x1-inch bars.

HINT : To crush candy or nuts, place in a zip-top plastic bag; seal bag and place on cutting board. Press lightly with wooden mallet or rolling pin.

CHOCOLATE BUTTER BRICKLE BARS

1 1/2 cups all-purpose flour
3/4 cup brown sugar, firmly packed
1/2 cup butter or margarine, softened
1/2 teaspoon salt, divided
1 6-ounce package butterscotch chips
1/4 cup light corn syrup
2 tablespoons butter or margarine
1 tablespoon water
1 cup pecans, chopped
1 6-ounce package milk chocolate chips

Preheat oven to 375°. In a medium mixing bowl, combine flour, brown sugar, 1/2 cup butter and 1/4 teaspoon salt. Press mixture into a 13x9x2-inch pan. Bake 10 minutes or until golden.

While crust is baking, melt butterscotch chips, corn syrup, 2 tablespoons butter, water and 1/4 teaspoon salt in a small saucepan over low heat. Stir until smooth. Remove from heat and stir in pecans. While crust is still warm, spread mixture over top of crust. Allow to cool completely. Melt chocolate chips and spread over butterscotch layer. Chill 10 minutes or until chocolate is set. Makes 32 bars.

COFFEE SPICE BARS

1 cup shortening
2 cups brown sugar
2 eggs
2 cups raisins
1/2 cup walnuts, optional
3 cups flour
1/2 teaspoon salt
1 teaspoon baking powder
1 teaspoon cinnamon
1 cup hot coffee

Barely cover raisins with water and boil until water is gone. Cream shortening and brown sugar. Add eggs and mix well. Add raisins. Mix dry ingredients and add to mixture. Mix well, then add hot coffee until well blended. Grease 2 9x13-inch pans. Spread mixture into pans. Bake at 325° for 25 minutes. Remove and cool before icing.

Icing:

3 tablespoons butter
2 cups powdered sugar
2 teaspoons vanilla
Enough coffee to make of spreading consistency

Mix well and spread on cooled bars.

CHOCOLATE TRIANGLES

2 squares chocolate
1/2 cup butter
1 cup sugar
1 cup flour
1/4 teaspoon salt
2 eggs, well beaten
1 teaspoon vanilla

Melt chocolate and butter. Stir in sugar , flour and salt. Add eggs and vanilla. Spread on well-greased cookie sheet. Sprinkle with chopped nuts. Bake at 400° for 10 minutes. Cut into triangles while warm.

GLAZED CINNAMON BARS

1 cup butter
1 cup brown sugar
1 egg, separated
Dash of salt
1 3/4 cups all-purpose flour
3 teaspoons cinnamon
1/2 cup powdered sugar
1/2 to 1 cup walnuts, chopped

Combine butter, sugar, egg yolk and salt. Beat until creamy. Stir in flour and cinnamon. Mix well. Spread thick batter into lightly greased 15x10-inch pan. Beat egg white until foamy. Stir in powdered sugar. Brush sugar mixture over batter. Sprinkle with walnuts. Bake in 350° oven 30-35 minutes. While hot, cut into 48 bars. Remove from pan and cool on rack.

DOUBLE DELICIOUS COOKIE BARS

1/2 cup margarine or butter
1 1/2 cups graham cracker crumbs
1 14-ounce can sweetened condensed milk
1 12-ounce package chocolate chips
1 cup peanut butter chips

Preheat oven to 350° (325° for glass pan). In 9x13-inch pan melt margarine or butter in oven. Sprinkle graham cracker crumbs over margarine; pour sweetened milk evenly over crumbs. Top with chips and press down firmly. Bake 25-30 minutes until golden brown. Cool. Cut into bars. Store loosely covered at room temperature.

HINT: Melt 1 cup chocolate chips with 1 1/2 teaspoon shortening and drizzle over bars. To make cone for drizzling, roll waxed or parchment paper into cone shape leaving a small opening at one end. Spoon chocolate or frosting into cone and squeeze onto bars or cookies. (And there's nothing to wash!)

CINNAMON STICKS

1 cup butter
3/4 cup sugar
2 cups flour
4 teaspoons cinnamon
1 large egg, separated
1 teaspoon vanilla
1 cup pecans, chopped

Cream butter, sugar, vanilla and egg yolk. Add flour and cinnamon. Press into greased 13x9x2-inch pan. Spread <u>unbeaten</u> egg white over dough. Then press chopped nuts down into all. Bake at 350° for 30 minutes. Cut into long narrow rectangles while warm.

FROSTED APPLE BARS

This is Cyndi's favorite cookie when the apples are ready in the fall.

Crust:

>2 1/2 cups flour
>1/2 teaspoon salt
>1 cup shortening
>2 egg yolks plus enough milk to make 2/3 cup

Mix flour, salt and shortening like pie crust. Add egg yolks and milk to form dough. Pat <u>half</u> of dough into 15x10-inch jelly roll pan. Prepare filling.

Filling:

>1 cup crushed corn flakes
>8 apples, sliced thin
>1 1/2 cups sugar
>1/2 teaspoon cinnamon
>2 egg whites, beaten until foamy

Spread corn flakes over crust. Spread apple slices evenly over corn flakes. Mix sugar and cinnamon together and sprinkle over apples.
Roll out remainder of crust and place on top of apples. Brush with egg whites. Bake at 350° for 1 hour. Glaze.

Glaze:

>1 cup powdered sugar
>3 tablespoons water
>1 tablespoon butter

Melt butter in microwave. Add water. Mix in powdered sugar. Spread over bars. Cool thoroughly before cutting into squares or triangles.

CHOCOLATE CARMELITA BARS

1 3/4 cups quick or regular oats
1 1/2 cups all-purpose flour
3/4 cup brown sugar, packed
3/4 cup margarine, melted
1 tablespoon water
1/2 teaspoon baking soda
1/4 teaspoon salt, optional
1 cup nuts, chopped
1 cup semisweet chocolate chips
1 cup caramel ice cream topping
1/4 cup all-purpose flour

Heat oven to 350°. Grease 13x9-inch baking pan. Combine first seven ingredients; mix well. Reserve 1 cup; press remaining onto bottom of prepared pan. Bake 10-12 minutes or until light brown. Cool 10 minutes. Top with nuts and chocolate chips. Mix caramel topping and 1/4 cup flour until smooth. Drizzle over chocolate pieces to within 1/4-inch of pan edges. Sprinkle with reserved oat mixture. Bake additional 18-20 minutes or until golden brown. Cool completely. Cut into 32 bars.

BROWNIE CHEESECAKE BARS

1 1/2 cups all-purpose flour
1 1/2 cups sugar
2/3 cup butter or margarine, melted
2/3 cup cocoa
3 eggs, divided
1/2 cup milk
3 teaspoons vanilla, divided
1/2 teaspoon baking powder
1 cup nuts, chopped, optional
1 8-ounce package cream cheese, softened
2 tablespoons butter or margarine
1 tablespoon cornstarch
1 can sweetened condensed milk

Heat oven to 350°. Grease 13x9-inch baking pan. In mixing bowl, beat flour, sugar, butter, cocoa, 2 eggs, milk, 2 teaspoons vanilla and baking powder until well blended. Stir in nuts. Spread into pan.

In small mixing bowl, beat cream cheese, 2 tablespoons butter and cornstarch until fluffy. Gradually add sweetened condensed milk, then remaining egg and 1 teaspoon vanilla, beating until smooth. Pour over brownie batter. Bake 35-40 minutes or until top is lightly browned. Cool. Cut into bars. Store covered in refrigerator. Makes 24-36 bars depending on size of cutting.

MILK CHOCOLATE AND PEANUT BUTTER BARS

1 cup peanut butter
6 tablespoons butter, softened
1 1/4 cups sugar
3 eggs
1 teaspoon vanilla
1 cup flour
1/4 teaspoon salt
1 11-ounce package milk chocolate chips

Preheat oven to 350°. In large mixing bowl, combine peanut butter and butter. Beat until smooth. Add sugar, eggs and vanilla. Beat until creamy. Blend in flour and salt. Stir in 1 cup chocolate chips. Spread into 13x9-inch baking pan. Bake 25-30 minutes or until edges begin to brown. Remove and sprinkle with remaining chocolate chips. Let stand 5 minutes until chips become shiny and soft. Spread chocolate evenly over top. Cool completely. Cut into 1 1/2-inch bars. Makes 48 bars.

COCONUT CHRISTMAS DIAMONDS

6 tablespoons butter, softened
1/4 cup granulated sugar
1/4 teaspoon salt
1 cup all-purpose flour, sifted
2 eggs
1 cup brown sugar
2 tablespoons all-purpose flour
1 teaspoon vanilla
1/2 teaspoon salt
1 cup flaked coconut
1/2 cup walnuts, coarsely chopped

Preheat oven to 350°. Cream together butter, granulated sugar and salt. Stir in 1 cup flour. Pat onto bottom of 9x9x2-inch pan. Bake at 350° for 15 minutes or until lightly browned.

Beat eggs slightly. Add vanilla. Gradually add brown sugar, beating just until blended. Add 2 tablespoons flour and 1/2 teaspoon salt. Mix well. Stir in coconut and nuts. Spread over baked layer. Bake 20 minutes longer or until wooden pick comes out clean. Cool. Cut into diamonds. Makes 1 1/2 dozen.

CARAMELICIOUS FUDGE BROWNIES

1 package fudge brownie mix
20 caramels
3 tablespoons milk
1/2 cup semisweet chocolate chips
1/2 cup pecans, chopped

Prepare brownie mix according to directions, using high-altitude directions, if applicable. In small saucepan over low heat, melt caramels and milk, stirring until smooth. Immediately after removing brownies from oven, sprinkle with chocolate chips and pecans. Drizzle with caramel. Cool completely before cutting into 24 bars.

CHERRY BARS

1 package white cake mix
2 eggs, slightly beaten
1/2 cup Maraschino cherries, chopped
1/2 cup walnuts, chopped
3 tablespoons Maraschino cherry juice
2 tablespoons water

Combine all ingredients. Mix well and spread on a greased and floured 15x10x2-inch baking sheet. Bake at 350° for 20-25 minutes. Frost when cooled.

Icing:

1/3 cup butter, softened
3 cups powdered sugar
3 tablespoons cherry juice
2 tablespoons cream

Mix together until smooth and spread on bars.

CHOCOLATE PECAN PIE BARS

3 cups flour
2 cups sugar, divided
1 cup butter or margarine, softened
1/2 teaspoon salt
1 1/2 cups corn syrup, light or dark
6 ounces German sweet chocolate or 6 squares semi-
    sweet chocolate
4 eggs, slightly beaten
1 1/2 teaspoons vanilla
2 1/2 cups pecans, chopped

Grease bottom and sides of 15x10x1-inch pan. In large mixing bowl, beat flour, 1/2 cup sugar, butter and salt at medium speed   until mixture resembles coarse crumbs. Press firmly and evenly into pan. Bake at 350° for 20 minutes.

Melt syrup and chocolate in saucepan over low heat. Remove from heat. Stir in 1 1/2 cups sugar, then eggs and vanilla until blended. Stir in pecans. Pour filling over hot crust and spread evenly. Bake at 350° for 30 minutes or until filling is firm around edges and slightly soft in center. Cool in pan on wire rack. Makes 48 bars.

CARAMEL BROWNIES

1 14-ounce package caramels
2/3 cup evaporated milk
1 18 1/2-ounce German chocolate cake mix
3/4 cup butter, melted
1 cup pecans or walnuts, chopped
1 cup semisweet chocolate chips

In a saucepan, melt caramels with 1/3 cup evaporated milk over low heat. In a mixing bowl, combine cake mix, butter, 1/3 cup evaporated milk and nuts; mix well. Spread half the dough into a greased 13x9-inch pan. Bake at 350° for 10 minutes. Remove from oven; sprinkle chocolate chips over baked crust. Drizzle caramel mixture on top. With hands, form remaining dough into small pancakes and place over caramel mixture (these will not completely cover the caramel mixture). Bake for 20 minutes. Cool slightly before cutting. Makes 2 1/2 dozen.

COCONUT JELLY CHEESE BARS

1 1/4 cups butter or margarine, softened
1 cup shredded cheddar cheese
1/2 cup sugar
2 1/2 cups flour
3/4 cup brown sugar
1 4-ounce package coconut
1 10-ounce jar currant jelly

Combine 1/4 cup butter, 1/2 cup flour and brown sugar to make crumbs. Set aside. Cream butter, cheese and sugar in bowl. Add flour and mix until well blended. Pat into ungreased 9-inch square pan. Bake at 350° for 30 minutes. Remove from oven and spread with jelly. Sprinkle reserved crumbs over jelly. Top with coconut and return to oven for 15 minutes. Cool. Cut into 24 bars.

SCRUMPTIOUS CHOCOLATE LAYER BARS

2 cups semisweet chocolate chips
1 8-ounce package cream cheese
1/2 cup plus 2 tablespoons evaporated milk
1 cup walnuts, chopped
1/4 cup sesame seeds, optional
1/2 teaspoon almond extract
3 cups all-purpose flour
1 1/2 cups sugar
1 teaspoon baking powder
1/2 teaspoon salt
1 cup butter or margarine
2 eggs
1/2 teaspoon almond extract

Combine chocolate chips, cream cheese and evaporated milk in medium saucepan. Cook over low heat, stirring constantly, until chips are melted and mixture is smooth. Remove from heat. Stir in walnuts, sesame seeds and 1/2 teaspoon almond extract. Blend well; set aside. Combine remaining ingredients in large mixing bowl. Blend well on low speed until mixture resembles coarse crumbs. Press half the crumb mixture into greased 13x9-inch pan. Spread with chocolate mixture. Sprinkle rest of crumb mixture over filling. (If crumb mixture softens and forms a stiff dough, pinch off small pieces to use as topping). Bake at 375° for 35-40 minutes or until golden brown. Cool. Cut into 36 bars.

CHEWY BOHEMIAN BARS

First layer:

> 1/2 cup butter
> 1 cup flour

Combine ingredients. Pat into 9x12-inch pan. Bake at 350°
for about 10 minutes until light brown .

Second layer:

> 1/2 cup coconut
> 1 1/2 cups brown sugar
> 1 cup pecans, chopped
> 2 tablespoons flour
> 1/4 teaspoon baking powder
> 1/2 teaspoon salt
> 2 eggs, beaten
> 1 teaspoon vanilla

Combine all ingredients for second layer. Spoon over baked
crust and return to 350° oven. Bake 20 minutes more. Cool.

Frosting:

> 1 1/2 cups powdered sugar
> 2 tablespoons butter
> 2 teaspoons lemon juice
> 1/4 teaspoon lemon flavor
> 2 tablespoons orange juice

Beat all ingredients together (if more liquid is needed to make
spreading consistency, use either more lemon or orange juice
to thin). Spread on cooled layers. Sprinkle top with nuts, if
desired. Cut into squares.

CREAM CHEESE SQUARES

1/2 cup brown sugar
1 cup flour
1/2 cup walnuts or pecans
1/3 cup butter
8 ounces cream cheese
1/4 cup sugar
1 egg
1 tablespoon lemon juice
1 teaspoon vanilla

Mix first four ingredients until crumbly. Set aside 1/3 cup of
the crumb mixture. Pat into 8x8-inch pan. Bake at 350° for
12-15 minutes. Beat sugar and cream cheese until smooth.
Add all other ingredients. Pour over crust and sprinkle with remaining crumbs. Bake at 350° for 25 minutes. Cool. Cut
into squares and refrigerate.

CHOCOLATE WALNUT BARS

1 1/2 cups flour
3 tablespoons brown sugar
3/4 cup margarine or butter
3 eggs
1 cup corn syrup
2/3 cup sugar
5 tablespoons margarine or butter, melted
1 1/2 teaspoons vanilla
3 squares semisweet chocolate, coarsely chopped
1 1/2 cups walnuts, chopped

Heat oven to 350°. Mix flour and brown sugar in small bowl. Cut
in 3/4 cup margarine until mixture resembles coarse crumbs.
Press onto bottom of 13x9-inch baking pan. Bake 20 minutes or
until edges are lightly browned. Beat eggs, corn syrup, sugar, melted margarine and vanilla in small bowl until well blended. Pour
over crust. Sprinkle with chocolate and walnuts. Bake 30 minutes
or until filling is set. Cool in pan. Cut into bars. Makes 3 dozen.

RHUBARB BARS

Yummy with ice cream.

     1 cup flour, sifted
     3/4 cup oats
     1 teaspoon cinnamon
     1 cup brown sugar
     1/2 cup butter, melted
     4 cups rhubarb, cut up
     1 cup sugar
     1 cup water
     2 tablespoons cornstarch
     1 teaspoon vanilla

Crumble first 5 ingredients together; press HALF of mixture into an 8-inch cake pan. Cover with rhubarb. Cook remaining ingredients until very thick; pour over rhubarb. Sprinkle with remaining oatmeal mixture. Bake at 350° for 1 hour. Serve warm or cold. Makes 9 large bars.

TRIPLE TASTY FUDGE BARS

     1 15-ounce package fudge frosting mix
     1 18 1/2-ounce German chocolate cake mix
     1/4 cup water
     1 egg
     1/2 cup dairy sour cream
     1 6-ounce package semisweet chocolate chips

Prepare frosting mix as directed on package. Combine dry cake mix, 1/2 cup prepared frosting, water and egg. Stir by hand until cake mix is moistened. Mixture will be stiff. Pat into 13x9-inch pan, greased on bottom only. Beat sour cream into remaining frosting. Spread over base. Sprinkle with chocolate chips. Bake at 375° for 40-50 minutes. Top will be puffy. Chocolate chips do not melt. Cool. Cut in bars. (For low altitude, bake at 350°.)

KARIN'S FRUIT BARS

A special friend gave this recipe to Cyndi; she used to bring them to the doctor's office where we all worked. We would gain ten pounds on those days because we ate so many!

2 1/3 cups sugar
1 cup plus 3 tablespoons shortening
3 eggs
1/2 cup honey
2 tablespoons water
5 cups flour
1/2 teaspoon salt
4 teaspoons soda
3 teaspoons vanilla
3 teaspoons cinnamon
1 1/2 pounds dates
1 pound raisins
2 cups walnuts
1 egg
2 tablespoons milk

Mix all ingredients together, except last egg and the milk; dough will be very stiff. Chill dough for easier handling. Spread into 3 long rolls about 3/4 inch thick onto 1 or two cookie sheets. Beat 1 egg and 2 tablespoons milk together and brush on unbaked rolls. Bake at 325-350° for 18-20 minutes. Watch closely because the honey in the dough burns easily. Cut while warm-just as good cold. Makes lots. They freeze well.

BROWNIE MIX

Make these by the batch or for a crowd. Georgie has used this recipe for years. It is great to have on hand for a quick after-school treat!

> 6 cups flour
> 4 teaspoons baking powder
> 4 teaspoons salt
> 8 cups sugar
> 1 8-ounce can unsweetened cocoa
> 2 cups shortening

Cut all ingredients together in large mixing bowl until smoothly blended. Makes about 6 batches. If baking all at once will make 3 15x10x2-inch baking dishes-approximately 72 brownies.

To make one batch of brownies mix together:

> 2 eggs, beaten
> 1 teaspoon vanilla
> 2 1/2 cups Brownie Mix
> 1/2 cup nuts, chopped

Grease 8x8-inch pan. Spread batter in pan and bake at 350° for 20 minutes. Can be frosted or dusted with powdered sugar.

CHOCOLATE HAZELNUT SQUARES

1 cup butter or margarine
3/4 cup sugar
2 large eggs
3 cups all-purpose flour
2 1/2 cups hazelnuts

In a large bowl or food processor, beat butter and sugar with a mixer or whirl until fluffy. Add eggs; beat or whirl to blend well. Stir in flour, then beat or whirl until well mixed. For easiest handling, chill dough airtight at least 1 hour or up to 5 days. (If chilled dough is too hard to work with, let stand at room temperature until soft enough to roll or shape.)

Pour 2 1/2 cups hazelnuts into a 15x10-inch pan. Bake at 350° for 15-20 minutes or until nuts are light brown. Spread nuts on a towel; rub with towel to remove as much of the loose brown skins as possible. Lift nuts from towel, discard skins. Coarsely chop nuts. Let pan cool, wipe clean and add cookie dough pressing evenly over bottom and up sides of pan. Bake crust at 325° until golden brown, 20-25 minutes.

Filling:

5 large eggs
1 3/4 cups brown sugar, firmly packed
1 tablespoon flour
1 teaspoon vanilla
Roasted nuts
8 ounces semisweet chocolate, coarsely chopped

Meanwhile beat eggs, brown sugar, flour and vanilla. Sprinkle nuts and 8 ounces coarsely chopped semisweet chocolate over crust; pour egg mixture over nuts and chocolate. Bake on lowest rack at 325° until filling is set when gently shaken, about 25 minutes. Cool, then chill until cold, about 2 hours. Cut into 1 1/2 inch squares. If making ahead, wrap air tight and chill up to 3 days; freeze to store longer. Makes 5 1/2 dozen.

COCONUT PECAN CRESCENT BARS

1 8-ounce can quick crescent dinner rolls
14-ounce can sweetened condensed milk
1 10-ounce package coconut pecan or coconut almond
    frosting mix
1/4 cup margarine, melted

Preheat oven to 400°. Unroll crescent dough and place rectangles in ungreased 15x10-inch jelly roll pan. Gently press dough to cover bottom of pan. Seal perforations. Pour condensed milk evenly over dough. Sprinkle with frosting mix. Drizzle with margarine. Bake at 400° for 12-15 minutes until golden brown. Cool. Cut into 3-4 dozen bars.

CHESS SQUARES

2 sticks margarine, melted
1 1-pound box dark brown sugar
1 cup sugar
4 egg yolks
2 cups flour
2 teaspoons baking powder
1/4 teaspoon salt
1 cup nuts, chopped
1 1/2 teaspoons vanilla
4 egg whites
Powdered sugar

Blend margarine, sugars and egg yolks. Beat well. Sift flour, baking powder and salt together. Add to creamed mixture. Fold in nuts and vanilla. Beat egg whites until stiff. Fold into mixture. Batter will be very thick. Spread into greased and floured 13x9-inch pan. Bake at 350° for 30-45 minutes. Sprinkle with powdered sugar. Slice when cool. Makes 30 squares.

CREAM CHEESE BROWNIES

4 ounces German sweet chocolate
5 tablespoons butter or margarine
3 ounces cream cheese, room temperature
1/4 cup sugar
3 eggs
1 tablespoon flour
1/2 teaspoon vanilla
3/4 cup sugar
1/2 teaspoon baking powder
1/4 teaspoon salt
1/2 cup flour
1/2 cup nuts, chopped
1 teaspoon vanilla

Melt chocolate with 3 tablespoons of the butter over low heat, stirring constantly until smooth. Cool. Cream remaining butter with cream cheese until smooth. Gradually add 1/4 cup sugar. Blend in 1 of the eggs, 1 tablespoon flour and 1/2 teaspoon vanilla.

Beat remaining 2 eggs until light. Gradually beat in 3/4 cup sugar. Stir in baking powder, salt and 1/2 cup flour. Blend in chocolate. Stir in nuts and 1 teaspoon vanilla.

Spread half of chocolate batter in a greased 8 or 9-inch square pan. Spread cheese mixture over top. Drop remaining chocolate batter by tablespoonfuls over top. Swirl through batters with a knife to marbleize. Bake at 350° for 35-40 minutes. Cool in pan.

LEMON ICED AMBROSIA BARS

This recipe come from the kitchen of Jerry Minerich, author of <u>Mystic Mountain Memories</u>, a mother-son cookbook.

1 1/2 cups flour
1/3 cup powdered sugar
3/4 cup cold margarine or butter
2 cups light brown sugar, firmly packed
4 eggs, beaten
1 cup flaked coconut
1 cup pecans, finely chopped
3 tablespoons flour
1/2 teaspoon baking powder

Preheat oven to 350°. In medium bowl, combine flour and powdered sugar. Cut in margarine until crumbly. Press onto bottom of lightly greased 13x9-inch baking pan. Bake 15 minutes. Meanwhile, in large bowl, combine remaining ingredients, except icing. Mix well. Spread evenly over baked crust. Bake 20-25 minutes. Cool. Top with lemon icing and chill. Makes 36.

Lemon Icing:

2 cups powdered sugar
3 tablespoons lemon juice
2 tablespoons butter or margarine, softened

Combine all ingredients until smooth and spreadable. Add more lemon juice, if necessary

CRANBERRY SQUARES

1/2 cup butter or margarine
1 cup light brown sugar, firmly packed
1 cup sugar
2 eggs
2 teaspoons vanilla
2 cups all-purpose flour
2 teaspoons baking powder
1/2 teaspoon salt
1/2 teaspoon ground cinnamon
1 16-ounce can whole berry cranberry sauce
2/3 cup walnuts, finely chopped

Preheat oven to 350°. In a medium sized saucepan, melt butter over moderate heat. Remove from heat. Beat in sugars, eggs and vanilla. Stir in flour, baking powder, salt and cinnamon until thoroughly combined. Stir in cranberry sauce and walnuts. Grease and flour 15x10-inch pan. Spread batter evenly. Bake 35-40 minutes. Cool completely before removing.

SAUCY BARS

1/2 cup shortening
1 cup sugar
1 cup applesauce
2 cups plus 2 tablespoons flour, sifted
1 teaspoon soda
1/2 teaspoon salt
1/2 teaspoon cloves
1 teaspoon cinnamon
1 teaspoon nutmeg
1 cup seedless raisins
1/2 cup nuts, chopped
1 teaspoon vanilla

Cream shortening and sugar. Add applesauce and mix well.
Sift together remaining dry ingredients and add to creamed
mixture, mixing well. Stir in raisins, nuts and vanilla. Mix well.
Spread batter in greased 13x9-inch pan. Bake at 350° for 35-
45 minutes. Frost with thin coating of powdered sugar icing
while warm. Makes 2 dozen bars.

ORANGE-DATE BARS

1 cup dates, chopped
1/3 cup sugar
1/3 cup vegetable oil
1/2 cup orange juice
1 cup all-purpose flour
1/2 cup pecans, chopped
1 egg
1 1/2 teaspoons baking powder
1 tablespoon grated orange rind

Combine dates, sugar, oil and juice in a saucepan. Cook for 5
minutes to soften dates. Cool. Add remaining ingredients.
Spread into an sprayed 8x 8-inch baking pan. Bake at 350°
for 25-30 minutes. Cool before cutting. Makes up to 36 bars.

FROSTY STRAWBERRY SQUARES

1 cup flour
1/4 cup brown sugar
1/2 cup nuts
1/2 cup butter, melted
2 egg whites
2 tablespoons lemon juice
1 cup sugar
16-ounce package strawberries, partially thawed
1 cup whipped cream

Mix flour, brown sugar, nuts and butter. Loosely spread onto a cookie sheet. Bake at 350° for 20 minutes. Stir several times during baking period to maintain crumbly consistency. Sprinkle 2/3 of the crumbs in a 13x9-inch pan.

Combine egg whites, sugar, berries and lemon juice in bowl. Beat at high speed to make stiff peaks. Fold into whipped cream. Pour over crumbs in pan and sprinkle remaining crumbs on top. Freeze for 6 hours.

PINEAPPLE SECRETS

1 cup sugar
2 tablespoons cornstarch
2 1/2 cups crushed pineapple and juice
1 3/4 cups flour
1 cup brown sugar
1/2 teaspoon baking soda
1/2 teaspoon salt
1 1/2 cups rolled oats
3/4 cup butter or margarine

For filling, combine sugar and cornstarch in small pan. Add pineapple and juice. Cook over medium heat until thick; set aside. Combine flour, brown sugar, soda, salt and oats; cut in butter until mixture is crumbly. Place half of crust mixture in greased 13x9-inch pan; pat down firmly. Spread filling evenly on top; add remaining crust and pat down as firmly as possible. Bake at 400° for 25-30 minutes. Cool; cut into 20 bars.

Drop
Cookies

DROP COOKIES INDEX

AMARETTO COOKIES

These are the most melt-in-the-mouth Italian-style cookies--more like macaroons, actually. Brew up some espresso coffee and enjoy.

> 1/2 cup egg whites (3 eggs)
> 1 1/4 cups sugar
> 1/4 teaspoon salt
> 1/2 cup Amaretto liqueur
> 3 1/4 ounces flaked coconut
> 4 ounces almonds, finely chopped

Beat egg whites until stiff. Then gradually beat in sugar 1 tablespoon at a time, until stiff and glossy. Add salt. Gradually beat in Amaretto. Fold in coconut and almonds. Line pans with foil. Drop mixture by heaping teaspoons onto foil. Bake at 325° for 20 minutes. Cool cookies on foil. Store in airtight container. Makes 4 dozen.

CHOCOLATE SOUR CREAM COOKIES

> 1 cup sugar
> 1/4 cup butter, melted
> 2 eggs, well beaten
> 1 cup sour cream
> 2 cups flour, sifted
> 1 teaspoon soda
> 1/2 teaspoon salt
> 1/4 cup cocoa

Combine sugar, butter, eggs and sour cream. Mix well. Sift dry ingredients together. Mix alternately with sour cream mixture. Drop by teaspoonfuls onto greased cookie sheet. Bake at 375° for 10 minutes. Frost with powdered sugar frosting. Makes about 3 dozen cookies.

CHERRY DROP COOKIES

1 cup margarine
1 1/2 cups sugar
2 eggs
2 tablespoons milk
1 teaspoon vanilla
1 teaspoon almond extract
2 1/2 cups flour
1/2 teaspoon baking powder
1 teaspoon salt
Red and green candied cherries, halved

In large bowl, with an electric mixer, cream margarine and sugar. Add eggs, beat until fluffy. Add milk, vanilla and almond extract; mix well. Add flour, baking powder and salt; blend thoroughly. Drop by teaspoonfuls onto greased cookie sheet. Top each with a cherry half. Bake in preheated 375° oven for 10-12 minutes or until lightly browned.

LEMONADE DROPS

1 cup shortening
1 cup sugar
2 eggs
3 cups flour
1 teaspoon baking soda
1/2 teaspoon salt
1 6-ounce can lemonade concentrate, thawed

Cream shortening and sugar. Thoroughly beat in eggs. Combine flour, soda and salt. Add alternately with 1/2 the lemonade. Drop by teaspoonfuls on a greased cookie sheet. Bake at 375° for 15 minutes. Before removing from the cookie sheet, brush tops with the reserved 3 ounces of lemonade.

OATMEAL SCOTCHIES

1 1/4 cups all-purpose flour
1 teaspoon baking soda
1/2 teaspoon salt
1/2 teaspoon cinnamon
1 cup butter, softened
3/4 cup sugar
3/4 cup brown sugar, firmly packed
2 eggs
1 teaspoon vanilla or grated peel of one orange
3 cups quick or old fashioned oats, uncooked
1 12-ounce package butterscotch chips

Preheat oven to 375°. In small bowl, combine flour, baking soda, salt and cinnamon; set aside. In large mixing bowl, beat butter, sugar, brown sugar, eggs and vanilla or orange peel until creamy. Gradually beat in flour mixture. Stir in oats and chips. Drop by spoonfuls onto ungreased cookie sheets. Bake 7-8 minutes for chewier cookies; 9-10 minutes for crisper cookies. Makes about 4 dozen cookies.

WHITE CHRISTMAS COOKIES
(from a New York City school)

2 1/4 cups sifted flour
1 teaspoon baking soda
1 teaspoon salt
1 cup unsalted butter, softened
3/4 cup brown sugar, firmly packed
3/4 cup sugar
3 large eggs
1 teaspoon vanilla extract
12 ounces white chocolate, coarsely chopped
3/4 cup salted macadamia nuts, coarsely chopped
1 1/4 cups golden raisins

Preheat oven to 350°. Lightly grease 2 cookie sheets. Combine flour, baking soda and salt in medium bowl and set aside. Beat butter and sugars in large mixer bowl at medium speed until light and fluffy. Add eggs one at a time, beating well after each addition. Beat in vanilla. Beat in dry ingredients. Stir in chocolate, nuts and raisins. Drop by rounded teaspoonfuls onto prepared cookie sheets. Bake 8-10 minutes until light golden brown. Cool on wire racks. Makes 6 dozen.

FRUIT COCKTAIL COOKIES

This is a very moist cookie. Can use pineapple or apple-sauce instead of fruit cocktail.

1 cup shortening
1 cup brown sugar
1/2 cup sugar
2 cups fruit cocktail
1 cup nuts, chopped
3 eggs, beaten
4 cups flour
1/2 teaspoon soda
1 teaspoon baking powder
1/2 teaspoon salt
1 teaspoon cinnamon

Mix and drop by spoonfuls on greased cookie sheet. Bake at 350° for 25 minutes. Can frost with powdered sugar glaze, if desired.

BLACK & WHITES

2 1/4 cups flour
1 cup dark brown sugar, packed
3/4 cup sugar
1/2 cup unsweetened cocoa powder
1/2 teaspoon baking soda
1/4 teaspoon salt
1 cup salted butter, softened
3 large eggs
2 teaspoons pure vanilla extract
1 cup (5 1/4 ounces) semisweet chocolate bar, coarsely
    grated
1 cup (5 1/4 ounces) white chocolate bar, coarsely
    grated

Heat oven to 300°. Beat butter; add sugars to form grainy
paste. Add eggs and vanilla. Add dry ingredients and choco-
lates. Blend until combined. Don't over mix. Drop by rounded tablespoons onto ungreased pans. Bake 23-25 minutes.

CHOCOLATE YOGURT MELTS

1 16.5 ounce Devil's Food chocolate cake mix
1 8-ounce cup cherry yogurt
1 egg, slightly beaten
2 tablespoons margarine, melted
2/3 cup walnuts, chopped
1 6-ounce package semisweet chocolate chips
Walnut halves for garnish, optional

Preheat oven to 350°. Combine cake mix, yogurt, egg and
margarine in large bowl; beat until blended. Stir in walnuts and
chocolate chips Drop dough by rounded teaspoonfuls 2 inches
apart on ungreased cookie sheets. Garnish with walnut halves,
if you wish. Bake at 350° for 12-15 minutes or until cookies
are set. Cool on wire racks. Makes 7 dozen.

CHOCOLATE-DIPPED COCONUT MACAROONS

      4 large egg whites
      1 1/3 cups sugar
      1/2 teaspoon salt
      1 1/2 teaspoons vanilla
      2 1/2 cups sweetened flaked coconut
      1/4 cup plus 2 tablespoons all-purpose flour
      8 ounces fine-quality bittersweet chocolate, chopped

In a heavy saucepan, stir together egg whites, sugar, vanilla, salt, and the coconut. Sift in the flour. Stir until well combined. Cook over moderate heat, stirring constantly, for 5 minutes. Increase heat to moderately high and continue stirring and cooking for 3-5 minutes more, or until it is thickened and begins to pull away from the bottom and sides of pan. Transfer to bowl to cool slightly, then chill covered with plastic wrap, until just cold. Drop heaping teaspoons, 2 inches apart on buttered baking sheets. Bake in the middle of a preheated 300° oven for 20-25 minutes or until light golden brown. Transfer to rack to cool.

     Melt chocolate over water, stirring until smooth. Remove from heat and dip macaroons, coating them halfway and letting excess drip off. Transfer to foil lined tray and chill for 30 minutes to 1 hour, or until chocolate is set. Store in waxed paper layered containers in the refrigerator for 3 days. Makes about 30 macaroons.

CHOCOLATE NUT COOKIES

1 cup unsalted butter
1/2 cup brown sugar
1/2 cup sugar
1/4 cup molasses
2 eggs
1 teaspoon vanilla
2 1/2 cups flour
1 teaspoon baking soda
1/4 teaspoon salt
1/4 teaspoon nutmeg
1 1/2 cups cashews, chopped
1/2 cup semisweet chocolate chips

In large mixing bowl, beat together butter, sugars and molasses until fluffy. Beat in eggs and vanilla. Add flour, baking soda, salt and nutmeg. Stir in cashews and chocolate chips. Drop dough by well-rounded teaspoonfuls 2 inches apart on a baking sheet. Bake at 350° for about 10 minutes. Makes 36 cookies.

PECAN KISSES

1 egg white
1 cup brown sugar
1/4 teaspoon salt
1 1/2 cups pecans, coarsely chopped

Beat egg white until stiff but not dry. Add brown sugar and continue beating until well blended. Add salt and pecans. Drop on greased and floured cookie sheet. Bake 25 minutes at 275° until nicely browned.

ZUCCHINI COOKIES

3/4 cup shortening
2 eggs
1/2 cup sugar
1 cup brown sugar
3 cups flour
1 teaspoon baking powder
1 teaspoon baking soda
1 teaspoon cinnamon
1 teaspoon nutmeg
2 teaspoons vanilla
2 cups zucchini, finely ground
3/4 cup dates, chopped
1/2 cup nuts, chopped

Cream until fluffy shortening, eggs and sugars. Sift dry ingredients together; mix vanilla, zucchini, dates and nuts together. Add dry ingredients alternately with zucchini to creamy mixture. Drop by teaspoonfuls on slightly greased cookie sheet. Bake at 375° for 8-10 minutes. Cool 1 minute before removing from pan.

CREAMY LEMON MACADAMIA COOKIES

2 cups all-purpose flour
1/2 teaspoon baking soda
1/4 teaspoon salt
1 cup light brown sugar, packed
1/2 cup sugar
1/2 cup salted butter, softened
4 ounces cream cheese, softened
1 large egg
2 teaspoons pure lemon extract
1 1/2 cups (7 ounce) whole macadamia nuts, unsalted

Preheat oven to 300°. In a medium bowl combine flour, soda and salt. Mix well with wire whisk and set aside. In a large bowl blend sugars well with an electric mixer set at medium speed. Add the butter and cream cheese, and mix to form a smooth paste. Add the egg and lemon extract, and beat at medium speed until light and soft. Scrape down sides of bowl occasionally. Add the flour mixture and macadamia nuts. Blend at low speed just until combined. Do not overmix. Drop by rounded tablespoons onto ungreased cookie sheets, 2 inches apart. Bake 23-25 minutes. Immediately transfer cookies with a spatula to a cool flat surface. Makes 3 dozen.

CHEWY CHOCOLATE-PEANUT BUTTER COOKIES

1 1/4 cups butter or margarine, softened
2 cups sugar
2 eggs
2 teaspoons vanilla
2 cups all-purpose flour
3/4 cup cocoa
1 teaspoon baking soda
1/2 teaspoon salt
2 cups peanut butter chips

Cream butter or margarine and sugar until light and fluffy in large mixing bowl. Add eggs and vanilla; beat well. Combine flour, cocoa, baking soda and salt; blend into creamed mixture. Stir in peanut butter chips. Drop by rounded teaspoonfuls onto ungreased cookie sheet. Bake at 350° for 8-9 minutes. (Do not overbake. Cookies will be soft. They will puff during baking and flatten upon cooling.) Cool on cookie sheet until set, about 1 minute. Remove to wire rack to cool completely. Makes about 4 1/2 dozen.

KAHLUA COCONUT CHOCOLATE CHIP COOKIES

*Kahlua, with its coffee and molasses flavors, and coconut
make an interesting compliment to chocolate.*

> 2 1/4 cups flour
> 1 teaspoon baking soda
> 2/3 cup butter, softened
> 1/4 cup sugar
> 3/4 cup light brown sugar, firmly packed
> 1/3 cup Kahlua
> 1 4-serving size package vanilla-flavor instant pudding
>   mix
> 2 eggs
> 12-ounce package semisweet chocolate chips
> 1 cup pecans, chopped
> 1/2 cup flaked coconut

Mix together flour and baking soda; set aside. In a large mixing
bowl, combine butter, sugars, Kahlua and pudding mix. Beat
until smooth and creamy. Beat in eggs. Gradually blend in dry
ingredients, then add the chocolate chips, nuts and coconut.
Chill dough for 1-2 hours. Drop by rounded teaspoonfuls, or
form dough into walnut-sized balls, onto ungreased baking
sheets. Bake at 375° for about 9 minutes. Makes about 5
dozen.

CHOCOLATE MOUNTAINS

1 cup shortening
2 cups brown sugar
2 eggs, well beaten
2 1/2 teaspoons vanilla
3 1/2 cups flour, sifted
1 teaspoon salt
2 teaspoons baking powder
1 cup milk
4 ounces chocolate
2 tablespoons shortening
2 cups nuts, chopped
Frosting

Cream shortening and sugar. Add eggs and vanilla. Mix flour, salt and baking powder together. Add dry ingredients alternately with milk to the creamed mixture. Melt chocolate and 2 tablespoons of shortening in microwave; cool. Add to dough. Stir in nuts. Drop by teaspoonfuls onto lightly greased baking sheets. Bake at 350° for 12-15 minutes.

Frosting:

1/2 cup butter
3 ounces chocolate
1/4 teaspoon salt
3 cups powdered sugar
5 tablespoons evaporated milk
1 egg white, well beaten
1 teaspoon vanilla

Heat butter and chocolate in microwave. Add salt, sugar and milk. Beat until smooth. Stir in beaten egg white and vanilla. Continue to beat until cool and thick enough to spread.

GERMAN PECAN BRITTLES

1 cup shortening
1 cup sugar
1 cup brown sugar, firmly packed
2 eggs
2 cups all-purpose flour
1 teaspoon baking powder
1 teaspoon baking soda
1 teaspoon salt
1 cup corn flakes cereal, crushed
1 cup pecans, chopped
1 teaspoon vanilla

Cream shortening in large mixing bowl; gradually add sugars, beating well. Add eggs, beat well. Sift together flour, baking powder, soda and salt in medium mixing bowl. Add cereal and pecans, stirring to coat well. Add to creamed mixture, mixing until well blended. Add vanilla. Drop by teaspoonfuls 2 inches apart on greased and floured cookie sheets. Bake at 325° for 10-12 minutes. Makes 11 dozen.

APRICOT CRUNCHIES

1/2 cup brown sugar, firmly packed
1/2 cup margarine or butter, softened
1 teaspoon vanilla
1 egg
3/4 cup plus 2 tablespoons flour
1/2 teaspoon baking soda
1/4 teaspoon salt
3/4 cup quick cooking rolled oats
1/3 cup coconut
1/3 cup wheat germ
1/2 cup dried apricots, chopped
1 cup cornflakes

Heat oven to 350°. Grease cookie sheets. In large bowl, beat brown sugar and margarine until light and fluffy. Add vanilla and egg; blend well. Stir in flour, baking soda, salt, rolled oats, coconut, wheat germ and apricots; mix well. Stir in cornflakes. Drop by teaspoonfuls 2 inches apart onto greased cookie sheets. Bake at 350° for 8-10 minutes or until light golden brown. Cool one minute; remove from cookie sheets. Makes 3 dozen cookies.

ORANGE DELIGHT COOKIES

Topping:

> 2 teaspoons grated orange rind
> 1 cup powdered sugar
> 1/3 cup orange juice

Mix topping before mixing cookies and let stand.

Dough:

> 1 1/3 cups sugar
> 3/4 cup shortening
> 2 eggs
> 1 1/2 tablespoons grated orange rind
> 3 cups flour
> 1/2 teaspoon soda
> 2 teaspoons baking powder
> 1 teaspoon salt
> 1/4 cup sour milk
> 1/2 teaspoon vanilla
> 3/4 cup nuts, chopped, optional

Mix sugar, shortening and eggs until creamy. Sift together dry ingredients. Add orange rind, sour milk, vanilla and sifted dry ingredients. Add nuts, if desired. Drop by teaspoonfuls onto greased cookie sheet. Bake at 375° for 12-15 minutes. Remove cookies from oven and spoon on topping while still hot. Cool and serve. Makes 4 dozen.

CAMP LOOKOUT OATMEAL COOKIES

These go fast! You may want to double the recipe.

        1/2 cup sugar
        1/2 cup shortening
        1 egg, beaten
        1/4 cup milk
        1 cup rolled oats
        1/2 cup raisins
        1/2 cup walnuts, chopped, if desired
        1 cup flour, sifted
        1/4 teaspoon salt
        1/2 teaspoon cinnamon
        1/2 teaspoon soda

Cream sugar and shortening; add egg, milk, oats, raisins and nuts. Add sifted dry ingredients. Drop by small spoonfuls onto greased cookie sheet. Bake at 350°-375° for 10-15 minutes. Makes 3 dozen.

GUMDROP COOKIES

        2 eggs
        1 cup brown sugar
        1/2 teaspoon cinnamon
        1 cup flour
        Dash of salt
        1/4 cup nuts, chopped
        1/2 cup gumdrops (no black ones), cut in pieces

Beat eggs well. Add sugar and beat again. Sift flour with salt and cinnamon. Add nuts and gumdrops. Mix all with first mixture and beat well. Drop by spoonfuls on greased cookie sheets. Bake at 375° for 8-10 minutes. May also be baked in 9x9-inch pan and cut into squares while warm.

COCOA-MALLOW-COOKIEWICHES

1 cup sugar
1/2 cup butter or margarine, softened
1 teaspoon vanilla
1 egg
1 cup milk
2 cups flour
1/2 cup cocoa
1 1/2 teaspoons baking soda
1/2 teaspoon baking powder
1/2 teaspoon salt

Heat oven to 375°. Grease cookie sheet. In large bowl, combine sugar, margarine, vanilla and egg; blend well. Stir in milk. Lightly spoon flour into measuring cup; level off and add with remaining ingredients. Mix well. Drop by rounded teaspoonfuls, 2 inches apart onto cookie sheets. Bake at 375° for 7-9 minutes or until edges appear set. Cool one minute. Remove from cookie sheets to rack and cool completely.

Filling:

2 cups powdered sugar
1 cup marshmallow cream
1/4 cup shortening
3-4 teaspoons milk
1 teaspoon vanilla

In large bowl, combine all ingredients. Beat until light and fluffy for about 2 minutes. Place two cookies together, sandwich style, using approximately 1 tablespoon of filling. Store in tightly covered container. Makes 30 sandwich cookies.

CHOCOLATE DATE-NUT DROPS

Chopped dates give these chewy chocolate drop cookies an unexpected flavor.

> 1 cup flour
> 1/2 teaspoon baking soda
> 1/8 teaspoon salt
> 3/4 cup butter or margarine, softened
> 1/2 cup sugar
> 1/2 cup brown sugar
> 1 egg
> 1 teaspoon vanilla
> 2 ounces unsweetened chocolate, melted and cooled
> 1 cup pitted dates, chopped
> 1 cup walnuts, chopped

Preheat oven to 375°. In small bowl stir together flour, baking soda and salt. Combine thoroughly; set aside. In mixing bowl, combine butter and sugars; beat until fluffy and well blended. Beat in egg until fluffy. Add vanilla and chocolate. Mix well. Gradually add flour mixture until just blended. Stir in dates and walnuts. Drop by slightly rounded tablespoonfuls, placed slightly apart onto ungreased baking sheets. Bake until tops of cookies feel firm when touched lightly (8-10 minutes). Let stand for a minute or two, then cool on wire racks. Makes about 4 dozen 2 1/2-inch cookies.

CHRISTMAS FRUIT COOKIES

This recipe can be cut in half. <u>And</u> it still makes a lot of cookies!

2 sticks butter, softened
1 1/2 cups brown sugar, packed
2 eggs, beaten
2 1/2 cups flour, unsifted
1 teaspoon cinnamon
1 teaspoon baking soda
1 teaspoon salt
1 teaspoon vanilla
4 ounces candied red cherries
6 ounces candied green cherries
6 ounces candied pineapple
2 pounds pitted dates, chopped
1 cup whole pecans, chopped
1 cup whole walnuts, chopped
2 pounds filberts, whole

In large bowl, cream butter, sugar, eggs and vanilla. Mix well. Remove 3/4 cup flour. Sift 1 3/4 cups flour, cinnamon, soda and salt. Add to creamed mixture. Add reserved flour to candied fruit for easier handling. Add fruits and nuts to batter. Mix well. Drop by teaspoonfuls onto sprayed cookie sheets. Bake in preheated 275° oven for 15-20 minutes. Makes 15 dozen.

CRY BABIES

3/4 cup sugar
1 cup margarine
1 egg plus 1 yolk
1/2 cup molasses
1 cup hot water
2 teaspoons soda
3 1/2 cups flour
1 teaspoon ginger
1 teaspoon cinnamon
1/2 teaspoon nutmeg

Cream together sugar, margarine and eggs. Add molasses. Dissolve soda in hot water and add to sugar mixture. Add flour and spices and mix well. Chill dough at least 2 hours or overnight. Drop on ungreased baking sheet. Bake at 375° for 8-10 minutes.

Frosting:

1/4 cup buttermilk
1 egg
1 teaspoon vanilla
1/2 teaspoon almond extract
2 1/4 cups powdered sugar

Mix together and frost cookies.

AMARETTO APRICOT CHEWS

1 cup all-purpose flour
1 teaspoon baking soda
1 cup butter or margarine
3/4 cup brown sugar, packed
1/2 cup sugar
1 egg
1 tablespoon Amaretto*
2 1/2 cups regular or quick-cooking rolled oats
1 cup dried apricots, snipped
1/2 cup almonds, finely chopped

Stir together flour and baking soda and set aside. In a large mixing bowl, beat butter or margarine until softened. Add sugars and beat until fluffy. Add egg and 1 tablespoon Amaretto and beat well. Add flour mixture and beat until well mixed. Stir in oats, apricots and almonds. Drop rounded teaspoonfuls onto ungreased cookie sheets. Bake at 375° for 8-10 minutes or until done. Cool on cookie sheet for 1 minute. Remove and cool thoroughly. Drizzle frosting over cookies. Makes about 54 cookies.

Drizzle:

2 cups powdered sugar, sifted
2-3 tablespoons Amaretto*

Stir together powdered sugar and enough of the 2-3 tablespoons Amaretto* to make an icing of drizzling consistency. Drizzle over cookies.

*You may use almond extract and water instead of Amaretto. In dough, omit Amaretto and use 1/2 teaspoon almond extract and 1 teaspoon water. In icing, omit Amaretto and use 1/4 teaspoon almond extract and enough water (2-3 tablespoons) to make icing of drizzling consistency.

PINEAPPLE COCONUT COOKIES

A "taste of the Tropics".

    1 cup shortening
    1 1/2 cups sugar
    1 egg
    1 8 1/2-ounce can crushed pineapple, with juice
    3 1/2 cups flour
    1 teaspoon baking soda
    1/2 teaspoon salt
    1 cup flaked coconut
    1/2 cup nuts, chopped

Mix shortening, sugar and egg thoroughly. Stir in pineapple.
Measure flour by dipping or by sifting. Stir together flour, soda,
salt and coconut; blend in thoroughly. Mix in nuts. Chill at
least 1 hour. Heat oven to 400°. Drop by rounded teaspoons
onto lightly greased cookie sheets. Bake 8-10 minutes or until
no imprint remains when touched lightly. Makes about 5
dozen cookies.

V.V.C.'S (VICKI'S VOLLEYBALL COOKIES)

    2 1/4 cups flour
    1 teaspoon soda
    1 cup margarine, softened
    1/4 cup sugar
    3/4 cup brown sugar
    1 teaspoon vanilla
    1 small package instant vanilla pudding
    2 eggs
    1 12-ounce package chocolate chips (or 1/2 package of
    chocolate chips and 1/2 package peanut butter chips)

Mix flour and soda. Beat butter, sugar, pudding and vanilla until
creamy. Beat in eggs. Add flour mixture. Drop on slightly
greased cookie sheets. Bake at 375° for 8-10 minutes.

65

SPICY APPLESAUCE COOKIES

1 cup sugar
1/2 cup shortening
1 egg
1 1/2 cups unsweetened applesauce
2 teaspoons soda
2 1/4 cups flour
1/2 teaspoon ground cloves
1 teaspoon cinnamon
1/2 teaspoon salt
1 cup raisins
1/2 cup nuts

Sift together flour, spices and salt; set aside. Dissolve soda in applesauce. Cream together sugar, shortening and eggs. Add applesauce mixture. Stir in flour mixture, raisins and nuts. Blend well. Drop by teaspoonfuls onto greased baking sheets. Bake at 300° for 15 minutes. Makes 30 cookies.

PEANUT CRUNCH COOKIES

1 cup butter
2 cups brown sugar
2 eggs
2 cups flour
1 teaspoon soda
1 teaspoon cream of tartar
1 teaspoon vanilla
1 7 1/4-ounce can salted Spanish peanuts
2 cups oatmeal
1 cup corn flakes

Cream butter and sugar; add eggs and beat well. Add remaining ingredients. Drop by small spoonfuls onto greased baking sheets. Bake at 325° for 12 minutes or until light brown. Do not overbake.

LUCILLE'S SUGAR COOKIES

"Mom's sugar cookies are always so-o good (and sugar cookies aren't even my favorite cookies)."--Cyndi

1 cup powdered sugar
1 cup white sugar
1 cup shortening
2 eggs, beaten
1 cup cooking oil
1 teaspoon vanilla
1 teaspoon almond extract
1 teaspoon lemon juice
5 cups flour
1 teaspoon baking soda
1 teaspoon cream of tartar, heaped

Cream together sugars and shortening. Beat in eggs, oil and flavorings. Stir in flour, baking soda and cream of tartar until well blended. Drop onto lightly greased cookie sheets. Bake at 375° for 8-10 minutes.

MOIST 'N CHEWY PEANUT BUTTER COOKIES

3/4 cup peanut butter
1/2 cup shortening
1 1/4 cups light brown sugar, firmly packed
3 tablespoons milk
1 tablespoon vanilla
1 egg
1 3/4 cups all-purpose flour
3/4 teaspoon salt
3/4 teaspoon baking soda

Heat oven to 375°. Combine peanut butter, shortening, sugar, milk and vanilla in a large bowl. Beat at medium mixer speed until well blended. Add egg and blend. Combine flour, salt and baking soda. Add to creamed mixture at low speed. Mix just until blended. Drop by heaping teaspoonfuls 2 inches apart onto ungreased baking sheet. Flatten slightly in crisscross pattern with tines of fork (Can be dipped in sugar before crisscrossing.) Bake at 375° for 7-8 minutes or until set and just beginning to brown. Makes about 3 dozen cookies.

APPLESAUCE COOKIES

1 cup sugar
1/2 cup shortening
1 egg
1 1/2 cups unsweetened applesauce
2 teaspoons soda
2 1/4 cups flour
1 teaspoon ground cloves
1 teaspoon cinnamon
1/2 teaspoon salt
1 cup raisins
1/2 cup nuts

Cream together sugar, shortening and egg; add applesauce in which soda has been dissolved. Sift in flour, spices and salt. Add raisins and nuts. Drop several inches apart onto greased baking sheet. Bake at 300° about 15 minutes. Makes 2 1/2 dozen.

CARAMEL DROPS

2 cups brown sugar
1 cup shortening
3 eggs
1 cup milk
1 teaspoon vanilla
3 cups flour, sifted
1 teaspoon baking soda
Dash of salt

Cream sugar and shortening together. Add eggs and beat well. Add remaining ingredients in order listed; mix well. Drop by spoonfuls onto slightly greased cookie sheets. Bake at 350° for 8-10 minutes. Frost. Makes 4 dozen cookies.

Icing:

1/4 cup butter
2 tablespoons cold water
1 teaspoon maple flavoring
1 egg beaten
3 cups powdered sugar

Brown butter. Add water, flavoring, egg and enough powdered sugar to thicken. Mix well until smooth. Spread on warm cookies.

CHOCOLATE CHIP COOKIES

This is Georgie's favorite chocolate chip cookie recipe. Her family loves it!

> 2/3 cup shortening
> 2/3 cup margarine, softened
> 1 cup sugar
> 1 cup brown sugar, packed
> 2 eggs
> 2 teaspoons vanilla
> 3 cups flour
> 1 teaspoon soda
> 1 teaspoon salt
> 1 cup nuts, chopped
> 1 12-ounce package chocolate chips, semisweet or
>   milk chocolate

Heat oven to 375°. Mix thoroughly shortening, butter, sugars, eggs and vanilla. Blend in remaining ingredients. (For a softer, rounder cookie, add 1/2 cup flour.) Drop dough by rounded teaspoonfuls 2 inches apart onto ungreased baking sheet. Bake 8-10 minutes or until light brown. Cool slightly before removing from baking sheet. Makes about 7 dozen cookies.

For Salted Peanut Cookies: Substitute 2 cups salted peanuts for chocolate chips and chopped nuts. Before baking, flatten each cookie with bottom of glass that has been greased and dipped in sugar.

HINT: Keep a supply of cookie dough on hand in the freezer for fresh cookies in a jif. Both cookie dough and baked cookies can be frozen and stored from 9-12 months.

CHUNKY CHOCOLATE COOKIES

2 cups flour
1 teaspoon baking soda
1/2 teaspoon salt
1 cup margarine
3/4 cup brown sugar
1/2 cup sugar
1 teaspoon vanilla
1 egg
1/4 cup sour cream
1 cup nuts, broken
8 ounces chocolate chunks
1 cup shredded coconut

Mix together flour, soda and salt; set aside. Cream together margarine, sugars and vanilla. Blend in egg and sour cream. Add flour mixture to margarine mixture. Stir in nuts, chocolate and coconut. Drop by teaspoonfuls on baking sheets. Bake at 375° for 12 minutes. Makes about 4 dozen.

ROCKY ROAD COOKIES

1 stick margarine or butter
1 6-ounce package chocolate chips
1 1/2 cups flour
1 cup sugar
1 cup nuts, chopped
1/2 teaspoon baking powder
1/2 teaspoon vanilla
1/4 teaspoon salt
2 eggs
4 dozen miniature marshmallows

Heat margarine and 1/2 chocolate chips in saucepan over low heat, stirring frequently until melted. Cool. Mix remaining ingredients including other half of chocolate chips and chocolate mixture except marshmallows. Drop by rounded teaspoonfuls 2 inches apart on ungreased cookie sheet. Press 1 marshmallow in center. Bake 8 minutes at 400° or so until no indentation when touched. Makes 4 dozen.

GOLDEN CRUNCH COOKIES

1 cup margarine
1/2 cup crunchy peanut butter
1 cup sugar
2 tablespoons water
2 eggs
1 teaspoon vanilla
1 teaspoon burnt sugar flavoring
1 1/2 cups flour
1 teaspoon soda
3 cups oats

Cream together margarine, peanut butter, sugars, water, eggs and flavorings until light and fluffy. Add flour and soda. Stir in oats last. Drop by teaspoonfuls onto greased cookie pans. Bake at 350° for 12 minutes. (May be chilled and rolled into balls, then flattened with sugared glass.)

PEANUT BUTTER CHOCOLATE CHIP COOKIES

Georgie uses milk chocolate chips in peanut butter cookies-- she just likes the combination of flavors.

- 2 1/4 cups creamy peanut butter
- 2 cups margarine, softened
- 2 cups sugar
- 2 cups brown sugar, packed
- 4 eggs
- 2 teaspoons vanilla
- 5 cups flour
- 4 teaspoons baking soda
- 4 cups chocolate chips

Cream together peanut butter and margarine. Add sugars, eggs and vanilla. Stir flour and baking soda together in a separate bowl. Add to creamed mixture. Stir in chocolate chips. Drop 2 inches apart by rounded tablespoonfuls onto a greased cookie sheet. Bake at 350° for 10-12 minutes. Makes about 6 dozen large cookies.

No Bake Cookies

NO BAKE COOKIES INDEX

RUM BALLS

1/2 pound vanilla wafers, crushed
1 cup powdered sugar
2 tablespoons cocoa
1 cup pecans, chopped
1/2 cup white syrup
1/4 cup rum

Mix all together, form into balls, and roll in powdered sugar.

CASSEROLE COOKIES

1 package almond bark, any flavor (1 1/2 pounds)
3/4 cup chunky or creamy peanut butter
2 1/4 cups rice krispies
1 1/2 cups miniature marshmallows
1 1/2 cups dry roasted peanuts
1 teaspoon vanilla, if desired (not necessary)

Melt almond bark and peanut butter in 225° oven or microwave oven. When melted, add rice krispies, marshmallows, peanuts and vanilla. Stir well. Drop by teaspoonfuls onto waxed paper. Cool. Makes 60 cookies. May need to add a little more rice krispies/nuts toward end.

Note: Many of the recipes in the no bake section are more like candy than cookies--but how delicious!

BUTTERSCOTCH CLUSTERS

12-ounce package butterscotch morsels
12-ounce can peanuts
5-ounce can chinese noodles

Melt butterscotch morsels in double boiler. Add peanuts and noodles; mix. Drop from teaspoon onto waxed paper. Makes a lot!

CHERRY CANDY BARS

2 cups sugar
2/3 cup evaporated milk
Dash of salt
12-16 marshmallows
4-ounce package cherry chips
1 teaspoon vanilla
12-ounce package chocolate chips
3/4 cup peanut butter
9-10 ounces crushed peanuts

Boil sugar, milk, salt and marshmallows for 5 minutes stirring constantly. Add cherry chips and vanilla stirring until the chips are melted. Pour into buttered 13x9-inch pan. In double boiler, melt chocolate chips and peanut butter. Stir in peanuts. Pour mixture over cherry layer. Cool and cut into small pieces. Refrigerate.

DATE BALLS

1 cup sugar
1 1/2 cups dates, cut up
1 stick margarine
1 egg
1 teaspoon vanilla
1 1/2 cups nuts, chopped
2 cups rice krispies cereal

Cook together sugar, dates, margarine, egg and vanilla for 6-8 minutes, stirring continuously. Remove from heat and add nuts. Cool to lukewarm and add cereal. Shape into balls the size of a walnut. Roll in powdered sugar and let stand until firm. May be frozen.

PRALINES

1 cup sugar
1 cup light brown sugar
1/2 cup milk
1/4 cup light corn syrup
1 teaspoon vanilla
2 cups pecans, chopped, room temperature

Combine the first 4 ingredients in deep sauce pan. Cook to soft ball stage 240°. Remove and add vanilla and pecans. Beat hard for 1-2 minutes with a wooden spoon. Drop by spoonfuls onto waxed paper and let stand until firm. Makes 40 small pralines.

ORANGE BALLS

1 stick margarine, softened
1 box powdered sugar
1 small can orange juice, undiluted
12-ounce box vanilla wafers, crushed
1 small package coconut, 3/4 cup pecans, chopped, or
    a combination of both

To softened margarine, add sugar, orange juice, and crushed wafers. Add nuts and/or coconut. Mold into small balls and roll in powdered sugar. Place in refrigerator for 3 hours. Store in airtight container at room temperature or in refrigerator.

WORLD FAMOUS CANDY BARS

6 cups cornflakes
1 cup peanuts
1 cup corn syrup
1/2 cup sugar
1/2 cup brown sugar
1/2 cup peanut butter
1/2 package milk chocolate bark

Combine cornflakes and peanuts in large bowl. Combine syrup and sugars in sauce pan. Bring to a boil. Remove from heat and add peanut butter. Pour over cornflakes and peanuts mix. Spread in a buttered jelly roll pan. Pat down. Melt chocolate bark in microwave. Pour on top. Let cool and cut into squares.

CHOCOLATE COVERED NUTS

1 6-ounce package chocolate chips
1 6-ounce package butterscotch chips
1 tablespoon peanut butter
1 1/2 cups salted mixed nuts

Heat both kinds of chips and peanut butter in top of double boiler until blended. Pour over nuts. Mix to cover nuts. Drop by teaspoonfuls onto waxed paper. Refrigerate until firm. Makes 42 pieces.

ENGLISH TOFFEE

People will think you worked for hours! Simple and delicious!!

2 sticks margarine
1 cup sugar
3 tablespoons water
1 teaspoon vanilla
4 chocolate bars
Nuts, chopped, optional

Boil margarine, sugar and water to hard crack stage, about 12 minutes. A drop in cold water shatters. Add vanilla. Pour into a greased 13x9-inch pan. Lay chocolate bars on top. Spread gently to cover. Sprinkle with nuts. Chill and break into pieces. Keep covered and refrigerated.

HOLLY COOKIES

These are very quick and colorful for the Holidays.

> 36 large marshmallows, melted
> 1 cube margarine, melted
> 2 teaspoons vanilla
> 1 teaspoon green food coloring
> 4 1/2 cups frosted flakes
> Red hots

Combine first five ingredients. Stir to coat all pieces. Drop by teaspoonfuls onto waxed paper. Decorate with red hots.

KAHLUA COCOA BALLS

> 1/2 cup Kahlua
> 1/4 cup light corn syrup
> 1/3 cup candied cherries, chopped
> 1/3 cup golden raisins, chopped
> 1 cup powdered sugar, sifted
> 1/2 cup unsweetened cocoa powder
> 2 1/2 cups vanilla wafers, ground fine
> 1 cup pecans, finely chopped
> Choose any of these for coating: powdered sugar, cocoa powder, coconut, chopped or ground nuts

Combine Kahlua with syrup and fruits. Blend sugar, cocoa, crumbs and pecans. Combine mixtures. Shape into small balls. Roll in desired coating. Freeze or store in an airtight container. Makes 4 dozen.

RUM-COFFEE BALLS

1 cup chocolate chips, melted
3 tablespoons corn syrup
3 cups powdered sugar
1 cup pecans, finely chopped
1 teaspoon instant coffee
1/4 cup hot water
1/4 cup rum
3/4 cup vanilla wafers, crushed

Mix all ingredients together. Wait a few minutes until dough is firm enough to roll. Roll into small balls. NO COOKING NEEDED! Roll balls in chopped nuts or chocolate shots.

FUDGE NOUGATS

1 cup sugar
3/4 cup flour
1/2 cup margarine
1 15-ounce can sweetened condensed milk
1 cup chocolate chips
1 cup graham cracker crumbs
3/4 cup nuts, chopped
1 teaspoon vanilla
1 cup miniature marshmallows

In saucepan, combine sugar, flour, margarine and condensed milk. Bring to a boil, stirring constantly. Boil 1 minute. Remove from heat. Add remaining ingredients, except marshmallows. Mix well. Add marshmallows. Spread in buttered 12x8-inch or 9x9-inch pan. Cool. Cut into squares to serve.

MICROWAVE PEANUT BRITTLE

Surprisingly light and crunchy!

> 1 cup raw peanuts or regular unsalted peanuts
> 1/2 cup light corn syrup
> 1 cup sugar
> 1 teaspoon margarine
> 1 teaspoon vanilla
> 1/8 teaspoon salt, optional
> 1 teaspoon baking soda

In 2-quart casserole, combine peanuts, corn syrup and sugar.
Cook 7-8 minutes full power, stirring well after 4 minutes. Add
butter, vanilla and salt and cook on high for 2 minutes. Stir in
baking soda. Pour onto buttered cookie sheet. Spread thin.
Cool and break apart. Store in airtight container.

S'MORES FUDGE

> 3 cups semisweet chocolate chips
> 1 14-ounce can sweetened condensed milk
> 1/4 cup butter or margarine, cut in small pieces
> 2 1/2 cups miniature marshmallows
> 2 double graham crackers, coarsely broken

Grease 8-inch square baking pan or line with waxed paper. In
medium microwave-proof bowl, combine chocolate chips, milk,
butter and 2 cups marshmallows. Microwave on medium for 4-
5 minutes, or until chips are just melted, stirring twice.
Remove from microwave; stir until smooth. Pour mixture into
prepared pan; sprinkle evenly with graham crackers and
remaining 1/2 cup marshmallows, pressing them lightly into
fudge. Cover and refrigerate for 1 hour or until firm. Cut into
small squares. Store in airtight container or refrigerate. Makes
64 squares.

CHRISTMAS ROCKS

9 almond bark cubes (18 ounces)
1 12-ounce package chocolate chips
4 cups rice krispie cereal
1 12-ounce jar peanuts

Melt almond bark and chips in microwave; mix in cereal and peanuts. Drop by teaspoonfuls onto waxed paper. Let stand until set. Makes about 4 dozen.

ORANGE BALLS OLE'

2 3/4 cups vanilla wafers, finely crushed
2 1/2 cups powdered sugar
1 cup nuts, finely chopped
1/4 cup orange juice concentrate
1/2 cup butter, melted
Powdered sugar or coconut

Mix together vanilla wafer crumbs, 2 1/2 cups powdered sugar and nuts. Add orange juice concentrate and butter. Mix thoroughly. Shape into 1-inch balls and roll in powdered sugar or coconut. Makes 6 dozen.

ORANGE COCONUT/NUT BALLS

1 pound vanilla wafers, crushed
1 cube margarine, melted
1 box powdered sugar
1 cup nuts, chopped
1 6-ounce can frozen orange juice

Thaw orange juice and add all ingredients. Shape into balls and roll in grated coconut.

CHRISTMAS BAVARIAN MINTS

1 6-ounce package real milk chocolate chips
1 6-ounce package semisweet chocolate chips
1 can sweetened condensed milk
1 teaspoon vanilla
1 tablespoon butter
1 tablespoon peppermint extract

Melt the chocolate chips in microwave or double boiler and add condensed milk, vanilla, butter and peppermint. Beat well and fast as it will set quickly. Spread in 13x9-inch pan. Cool and cut into bars.

WHITE AND DARK CHOCOLATE TRUFFLE SQUARES

1 10-ounce package vanilla milk chips
1 tablespoon butter flavored shortening
1/3 cup whipping cream
2 tablespoons butter
1 cup semisweet chocolate chips
1/2 teaspoon vanilla

Line 8x8x2-inch pan with heavy duty foil. In small microwavable dish combine vanilla chips and shortening. Microwave on high for one minute or just until chips are melted and smooth when stirred. Pour 1/2 vanilla chip mixture into pan. Set aside remaining vanilla chip mixture.

In medium microwavable dish, combine whipping cream and butter. Microwave on high for 30 seconds to one minute, stirring every 30 seconds just until mixture starts to boil. Immediately stir in chocolate chips until melted. Continue stirring until mixture thickens and cools slightly. Stir in vanilla. Pour into pan over vanilla chip mixture. Chill 10 minutes.

Microwave remaining vanilla chip mixture at high for seconds or just until mixture is fluid. Pour and spread over chocolate layer. Before mixture firms up, cut through until layer are scored into 1 inch squares. Cover and chill until firm. Cut with sharp knife following score marks. Serve chilled. Makes 4 dozen.

FILBERT CONFECTION CREAMS

1 cup filberts, chopped
1/2 cup butter
1/4 cup sugar
2 tablespoons cocoa
2 teaspoons vanilla
1/4 teaspoon salt
1 egg
1 3/4 cups vanilla wafer crumbs
1/2 cup flaked coconut
Icing

Spread filberts in shallow pan; toast in 350° oven 5-10 minutes. Stir occasionally, until lightly browned. In saucepan, combine butter, sugar, cocoa, vanilla, salt and egg. Cook over low heat until mixture thickens and becomes glossy. Combine crumbs, filberts and coconut; add to cocoa mixture. Spread evenly in pan and frost. Makes 6 dozen cookies.

Frosting:

1/3 cup butter
1 egg
1/2 teaspoon peppermint extract
2 cups sifted powdered sugar
4 squares semisweet chocolate

Cream butter; add egg and extract, beating well. Beat in sugar until smooth and creamy. Spread over chocolate base. Chill until icing is firm. Melt chocolate over hot water; spread over icing. When partially set, cut into small oblong bars. Refrigerate until ready to serve.

Shaped
Cookies

SHAPED COOKIES INDEX

CHECKERBOARDS

1 cup unsalted butter or margarine (no spread)
1/2 cup sugar
2 teaspoons vanilla
2 1/4 cups flour
1/4 cup unsweetened cocoa powder

Beat butter, sugar and vanilla. Add flour just until blended. Split dough in half into two balls. Add color or cocoa to 1/2. Split balls in half for 4 balls. Roll balls into 11-inch ropes. Stack alternating colors. Press logs together. Turn to all 4 sides. Slice and place 1 inch apart on ungreased cookie sheet. Bake at 350° for 10 minutes. Makes 60 cookies.

CHECKERBOARD COOKIES

Here's another variation of this favorite cookie.

1 cup butter or margarine, room temperature
1/2 cup sugar
1 egg yolk
1 tablespoon grated orange peel
1 teaspoon vanilla
2 1/2 cups all-purpose flour
2 ounces unsweetened chocolate, melted

Preheat oven to 350°. Use greased baking sheets. Beat together first 5 ingredients until light and fluffy. Add flour gradually until well blended. Divide dough into 2 equal portions. Add melted chocolate to one portion, blending well. Shape chocolate dough into 4 logs 15 inches long and 1/2 inches in diameter. Roll plain dough in same manner. Place a plain and chocolate log side by side, then place a chocolate log and a plain log on top in checkerboard fashion. Press together lightly. Wrap and chill for at least 2 hours. Cut chilled dough into 1/2- inch slices. Bake at 350° for 8-10 minutes, or until plain dough is golden. Makes 9 dozen cookies.

CHOCOLATE-DIPPED COCONUT MACAROONS

    4 large egg whites
    1 1/3 cups sugar
    1/2 teaspoon salt
    1 1/2 teaspoons vanilla
    2 1/2 cups sweetened flaked coconut
    1/4 cup plus 2 tablespoons all-purpose flour
    8 ounces fine-quality bittersweet chocolate, chopped

In a heavy saucepan, stir together egg whites, sugar, vanilla, salt, and the coconut. Sift in the flour. Stir until well combined. Cook over moderate heat, stirring constantly, for 5 minutes. Increase heat to moderately high and continue stirring and cooking for 3-5 minutes more, or until it is thickened and begins to pull away from the bottom and sides of pan. Transfer to bowl to cool slightly, then chill covered with plastic wrap, until just cold. Arrange heaping teaspoonfuls of mixture, 2 inches apart on buttered baking sheets. Bake in the middle of a preheated 300° oven for 20-25 minutes or until light golden brown. Transfer to rack to cool.

    Melt chocolate over water, stirring until smooth. Remove from heat and dip macaroons, coating them halfway and letting excess drip off. Transfer to foil lined tray and chill for 30 minutes to 1 hour, or until chocolate is set. Store in waxed paper layered containers in the refrigerator for 3 days. Makes about 30 macaroons.

GINGER COOKIES

3/4 cup butter-flavor shortening
1 cup sugar
1/4 cup light molasses
1 egg
2 cups flour
1 teaspoon salt
1 teaspoon baking soda
1 teaspoon each cinnamon, cloves, ginger

Combine all ingredients in order given. Roll into balls and then roll balls in sugar. Place on slightly greased cookie sheet. Bake at 375° for 12 minutes. Frost if desired when cooled.

MARBLE COOKIES

1 cup butter or margarine
3/4 cup sugar
1 large egg
2 1/2 cups all-purpose flour
1 1/2 ounces semisweet chocolate chips

In a large bowl or food processor, beat butter and sugar with a mixer or whirl until well mixed. Beat in egg. Stir in flour, beating until well mixed. Melt chocolate over hot water or in the microwave. Pour over dough. With a knife or spatula, swirl chocolate partially through dough. Do not overmix or marbling effect will be lost. Shape into 48 equal balls, or chill dough to roll and cut into desired shapes. Place on ungreased cookie sheets and bake at 350° for 15-20 minutes. Remove to racks to cool. Makes 4-5 dozen cookies.

Chocolate dipped cookies: Make cutout cookies. Melt 16-ounce package semisweet chocolate chips. Dip each cookie halfway into chocolate (or spread chocolate over half of each cookie). Let chocolate drip off, then lay cookies on a rack. Let stand until chocolate is firm, about 1 hour. Serve, or package airtight up to 3 days; freeze to store longer.

Almond cookies: Make the basic dough and shape into 48 equal balls. Pour 2/3 cup sliced almonds into a small bowl. Press each cookie ball into nuts to coat 1 side. Place balls on baking sheet. Press with fingertips to flatten slightly. Bake, cool and store as directed for cutout cookies. If desired, seal 2 ounces semisweet chocolate chips or chunks in a small, unpleated zip-lock plastic bag. Melt chocolate in double boiler or microwave. Trim a corner from the bag to make a 1/8-inch hole. Pipe chocolate over cookies to decorate. Let stand until chocolate is firm. Store as directed. Makes 48.

Chocolate logs: Make basic dough; shape into 48 logs, 3 inches long. Bake as directed for cutout cookies. Cool. Melt 6 ounces semisweet chocolate chips. Dip both ends of the logs into chocolate to coat and then roll ends in 1/2 cup finely chopped walnuts or pecans. Set on rack until chocolate is firm. Store as directed.

Tree cookies: Make basic dough, omitting egg and granulated sugar; add 1 cup firmly packed brown sugar. If necessary squeeze dough between your hands until it sticks together. Pat dough into a 12 x 15 inch pan into a 5 x 14 inch rectangle. On a 14 inch side, mark edge of dough at 2 inch intervals. On the opposite side, make the first mark at 1 inch, then every 2 inches. With a knife, score across dough from the 1 inch mark to the top opposite corner, then score from the 1 inch mark to the first 1 inch mark; repeat until you have 13 triangles plus 2 narrow end pieces. Cut off the end pieces; press the dough together and divide into 13 equal pieces. Press each piece onto a wide end of each triangle shaping it like a tree trunk. Bake at 300° until cookies are golden brown, about 40 minutes. While cookies are warm, cut through score marks. Let cool on baking sheet. To decorate, melt 2 ounces semisweet chocolate chips and pipe over the triangle portion of each tree.

CHRISTMAS COOKIES

Use this basic dough and quick, simple changes in flavors, shapes and decorations to make a variety of Christmas cookie treats.

> 1 cup butter or margarine
> 3/4 cup sugar
> 1 large egg
> Flavor and shape variations (choices follow)
> 2 1/2 cups all-purpose flour

In a large bowl or food processor, beat butter and sugar with a mixer or whirl until fluffy. Add egg and flavoring; beat or whirl to blend well. Stir in flour, then beat or whirl until well mixed. For easiest handling, chill dough airtight at least 1 hour or up to 5 days. (If chilled dough is too hard to work with, let stand at room temperature until soft enough to roll or shape.)

Flavor, shape and bake, using the choices that follow. Cool cookies on racks. When cool. Serve or immediately package airtight. Chill up to 3 days; freeze to store longer.

Cutout shapes: Roll dough until 1/4 inch thick, a portion at a time, on a generously floured surface. Cut into desired cookie cutter shapes. Place on ungreased baking sheet. Bake 15-20 minutes at 350°. Repeat until all the dough is used. Remove to racks to cool. Makes 4-5 dozen 2-3 inch cookies.

Spice shapes: To basic dough add 2 teaspoons ground cinnamon, 1 teaspoon ground ginger and 1/2 teaspoon ground nutmeg to the flour. Continue as directed for cutout cookies.

Chocolate shapes: Change basic dough by reducing flour to 2 cups, increasing sugar to 1 cup, adding 3 tablespoons unsweetened cocoa powder. Continue as directed for cutout shapes.

CHRISTMAS ALMOND TARTS

1 cup butter or margarine
3/4 cup sugar
2 large eggs
3 cups all-purpose flour

In large bowl or food processor, beat butter and sugar with a mixer or whirl until fluffy. Add eggs; blend well. Stir in flour, then beat or whirl until well mixed. Chill dough for 1 hour for easier handling. Divide dough equally among 72 miniature (1 - 1 1/2 inch) tart pans; press dough evenly over bottom and sides of pans (keep unused dough and filling chilled). Set pans close together on 12 x 15-inch baking sheets.

Filling:

1 cup almond paste
3 tablespoons flour
3 tablespoons sugar
2 large eggs
2 large egg whites
1/2 teaspoon almond extract

In a food processor or bowl, whirl or beat almond paste, flour and sugar until fine crumbs form. Add eggs, 1 at a time, egg whites and almond extract. Whirl or beat until smooth. Spoon 1 teaspoon filling into each tart pan. Bake at 325° until tops are golden brown, about 30 minutes. Cool 5 minutes.

Frosting:

1 cup powdered sugar
2 tablespoons milk

Smoothly mix powdered sugar and milk. Spoon about 1/4 teaspoon of the mixture on top of each warm tart. If icing stands while you bake tarts in batches, stir to make smooth and add a few drops of milk to maintain a smooth consistency. When tarts are cool, remove from pans; use the tip of a small, sharp knife, if needed, to help loosen pastry. Serve, or chill airtight up to 2 days; freeze to store longer. Makes 6 dozen.

CHOCOLATE-CARAMEL SUGAR COOKIES

We won't try to figure out how many calories are in these!

Cookies:

>3 squares unsweetened chocolate
>1 cup margarine or butter
>1 cup sugar
>1 egg
>1 teaspoon vanilla
>2 cups all-purpose flour
>1 teaspoon baking soda
>1 teaspoon salt
>1 cup nuts, finely chopped

Microwave chocolate and margarine in large microwaveable bowl on high for 2 minutes or until margarine is melted. Stir sugar into chocolate mixture until well blended. Stir in egg and vanilla and completely mix. Mix in flour, soda and salt. Refrigerate 10 minutes. Heat oven to 375°. Shape dough into 1 inch balls; roll in nuts. Make indentation in each ball. Place on ungreased cookie sheets. Bake for 8-10 minutes or until set. Remove from cookie sheets to cool on wire racks. Makes about 3 1/2 dozen.

Filling/Topping:

>1 square unsweetened chocolate
>1 14-ounce package caramels
>2 tablespoons milk

Microwave caramels with 1 tablespoon milk in microwaveable dish on high 3 minutes or until melted, stirring after 2 minutes. Fill center of cookies with caramel mixture. Place chocolate in zipper-style sandwich bag. Close bag tightly. Microwave on high about 1 minute or until chocolate is melted. Fold down top of bag tightly and snip about 1/8 inch off one corner. Holding top of bag tightly, drizzle chocolate through opening over cookies.

CRISP POTATO CHIP COOKIES

1 cup butter or margarine, softened
1 cup sugar
1 cup light brown sugar
2 eggs
1 6-ounce package semisweet chocolate pieces
1/2 cup nuts, chopped
2 cups potato chips, crushed
2 cups flour
1 teaspoon baking soda

Mix flour and soda; set aside. Beat butter, sugars and eggs until well blended. Stir in chocolate, nuts, potato chips and flour mixture until well blended. Shape in 3/4 inch balls and place 2 inches apart on greased cookie sheet. (If dough is too sticky, chill about 1/2 hour or until firm enough to handle.) Bake in preheated 350° oven until light brown, 10-12 minutes. Cool 1/2 minute on cookie sheet and remove to wire rack; cool completely. Makes about 84. Store in airtight container in cool dry place; will keep about 2 weeks.

FANCY SCOTCH SHORTBREAD

3/4 cup butter or margarine
1/4 cup sugar
2 cups flour

Mix butter and sugar thoroughly. Measure flour by dipping method or by sifting. Work in flour with hands. Chill dough. Heat oven to 350°. Roll dough 1/3-1/2-inch thick. Cut into fancy shapes. Flute edges, if desired, by pinching between fingers as for pie crust. Place on an ungreased baking sheet. Bake for 20-25 minutes. (The tops do not brown during baking, nor do the shapes of the cookies change.) Makes about 2 dozen cookies. Try tinting the dough before chilling it.

GINGERSNAP COOKIES

1 cup sugar
3/4 cup shortening
1 egg
2 tablespoons dark corn syrup
2 tablespoons molasses
2 cups flour
1 teaspoon cinnamon
1/2 teaspoon nutmeg
2 teaspoons baking soda
1 teaspoon ginger
1/2 teaspoon cloves

Beat sugar, shortening, egg, syrup and molasses together. Add remaining ingredients and mix well. Make into balls. Roll in sugar. Place on lightly greased cookie sheets. Bake at 375° for 8-10 minutes until plump.

MOCHA PECAN BALLS

2 sticks (1 cup) unsalted butter, softened
1/2 cup sugar
2 teaspoons vanilla
1 tablespoon instant espresso powder
1/4 cup unsweetened cocoa powder
3/4 teaspoon salt
1 3/4 cups all-purpose flour
2 cups pecans, finely chopped
Powdered sugar for coating the cookies

In a bowl with an electric mixer, cream the butter with the sugar until the mixture is light and fluffy. Add the vanilla, espresso powder, cocoa powder, and salt. Beat the mixture until it is combined well. Add the flour; beat the dough until it is just combined and stir in the pecans. Chill the dough, covered, for at least 2 hours or overnight. Preheat the oven to 375°. Roll the dough into 1-inch balls and arrange the balls about 1 inch apart on baking sheets. Bake the cookies in batches in the middle of the oven for 12-15 minutes or until they are just firm. Let them cool for 5 minutes on the sheets. Toss the warm cookies in a bowl of powdered sugar to coat them well. The cookies may be made 2 months in advance and kept frozen in airtight containers. Makes about 95 cookies.

CARAMEL COOKIES

3/4 cup brown sugar, firmly packed
1 cup butter, softened
1 egg yolk
2 cups flour

Mix sugar and butter until fluffy. Add egg yolk. Stir in flour. Refrigerate, if necessary for easier handling. Shape dough into 1-inch balls and flatten with fork. Bake at 325° for 10-12 minutes until golden brown.

SUGARED ALMOND CRESCENTS

1 cup tub margarine
1/3 cup sugar
2/3 cup ground blanched almonds
1 2/3 cups enriched, all-purpose flour
1/4 teaspoon salt
1/2 cup powdered sugar
1/2 teaspoon ground cinnamon

Preheat oven to 325°. Mix margarine, sugar, and almonds thoroughly. Work in the flour and salt. Chill dough 2-3 hours. Roll dough, a small portion at a time, with hands until pencil thick. Cut into 2 1/2 inch lengths and shape into crescents on an ungreased baking sheet. Bake for 15 minutes or until set but not browned. Cool on baking sheet for a few minutes. While still warm, carefully dip in mixture of confectioners sugar and cinnamon. Makes 48 cookies.

Hint: Although it works well in this recipe, do not use tub margarine, margarine blends or low fat spreads in your cookies. It alters the texture of the cookies.

RAISIN PUFF COOKIES

1 cup water
1 1/2 cups raisins
1 1/2 cups sugar
1 cup shortening
3 eggs
3 1/2 cups flour
1 teaspoon soda
1 teaspoon salt.

Boil raisins in water until water is absorbed; cool. Cream together sugar and shortening. Add eggs and mix well. Sift together flour, soda and salt and add to mixture. Stir in raisins and mix well. Ball small amount of dough in hand (walnut size). Roll in sugar and place on a greased cookie sheet. Do not press dough down. Bake at 350 degrees for 15 minutes or until light brown. Dough may be chilled overnight.

CHOCOLATE-ORANGE CUPS

1 cup almonds, finely chopped
3/4 cup powdered sugar
1/4 cup unsweetened cocoa powder
2 teaspoons orange peel, finely grated
8 tablespoons regular stick butter or margarine, at room
     temperature
3 large egg whites
1 tablespoon sugar
2 squares semisweet chocolate, melted and cooled
1 teaspoon vegetable oil
2 tablespoons almonds for garnish, coarsely chopped

Heat oven to 350°. Arrange twenty 1 1/2-inch foil baking
cups on a cookie sheet. In a small bowl, mix almonds, powdered sugar, cocoa and orange peel. Stir in 6 tablespoons of
the butter and 1 egg white. In a small bowl, beat remaining
egg whites with electric mixer until foamy. Add sugar. Beat
just until stiff peaks form when beaters are lifted. Fold into
almond mixture. Fill baking cups 3/4 full. Bake 13 to 16 minutes until tops look dry. Cool on cooking sheet. Meanwhile,
mix remaining 2 tablespoons butter and melted chocolate. Stir
in oil. Spread mixture on cookies and sprinkle with chopped
almonds. Store airtight in the refrigerator up to three weeks.
Makes 20 to 24 cookies.

SUGAR COOKIES

1 1/2 cups powdered sugar, sifted
1 cup margarine
1 egg
1 teaspoon vanilla
1/2-1 teaspoon almond flavoring
2 1/2 cups flour, sifted
1 teaspoon soda
1 teaspoon cream of tartar

Preheat oven to 375°. Cream sugar and margarine then add other ingredients. Refrigerate 2-3 hours. Divide dough in half and roll out on lightly floured surface to 3/16 inch thick. Cut into desired cookie shapes. Sprinkle with sugar or frost when cool. (Also good left plain.) Place on lightly greased baking sheet. Bake 7-8 minutes, or until lightly brown.

MOM'S SUGAR COOKIES

1 cup shortening
3 eggs
1 teaspoon vanilla
1 1/2 cups sugar
1 1/2 teaspoons baking powder
2-3 cups flour

Preheat oven to 400°. Mix above ingredients. Roll out. Cut out. Bake for 6-10 minutes on lightly greased baking sheets.

POPPY SEED COOKIES

Use the food processor for this recipe.

1 cup sugar
Peel of one orange
1 egg yolk
1 cup unsalted butter
1/2 teaspoon salt
1/2 teaspoon nutmeg
1 cup unbleached flour
1 cup cake flour
1/4 cup poppy seeds

Blend sugar and orange peel in food processor using an off and on motion. Add yolk. Blend in butter, salt and nutmeg. Again with off and on motion mix in the flours and poppy seed, being careful not to over process. Divide into equal portions and form into logs. Wrap and refrigerate until firm. Slice 1/4 inch and place 1 1/2 inches apart on cookie sheet. Bake at 350° for about 8 minutes. Makes 5 dozen.

FANCY TEA COOKIES

1/2 cup butter
1/2 cup shortening
3 tablespoons sugar
1 teaspoon vanilla
2 cups flour
1 cup coconut

Combine butter, shortening and sugar, creaming until light and fluffy; add vanilla. Work in flour and coconut gradually until well blended. Form 2 rolls; chill in refrigerator overnight. Slice dough 1/4-inch thick. Slices may be cut in fancy shapes. Bake at 275° for 35-45 minutes.

THUMBPRINT COOKIES

1/2 cup shortening (part butter or margarine)
1/4 cup brown sugar, packed
1 egg, separated
1/2 teaspoon vanilla
1 cup flour
1/4 teaspoon salt
3/4 cup finely chopped nuts
Jelly or tinted powdered sugar icing

Heat oven to 350°. Mix shortening, sugar, egg yolk, and vanilla thoroughly. Measure flour by dipping method or by sifting. Blend together flour and salt; stir into mixture. Roll dough into balls (1 teaspoon per ball). Beat egg white slightly with fork. Dip balls in egg white. Roll in nuts. Place about 1 inch apart on ungreased baking sheet; press thumb gently in center of each. Bake 10-12 minutes, or until set. Cool. Fill thumbprint with jelly or tinted icing. Makes about 3 dozen cookies.

1 stick margarine, softened
1 cup sugar
1 egg
1 teaspoon almond extract
1 2 3/4-ounce package instant potatoes
1 1/2 cups Bisquick
Almond slices, optional

Cream margarine; add sugar gradually. Beat in egg and almond extract. Add instant potato flakes and Bisquick, beating until well mixed. Roll dough into marble-size pieces; make slight indentation in top. Bake on greased cookie sheet at 350° approximately 12 minutes. A sliced almond may be pressed into each cookie before baking. Makes 6 dozen.

MISTLETOE BONBONS

1/2 cup margarine
3/4 cup powdered sugar, sifted
1 tablespoon vanilla
1 1/2 cups flour
1/8 teaspoon salt
Chocolate kisses for center
Food color
Icing: plain and chocolate
Toppings: nuts, coconut, colored sugar

Mix butter, sugar, vanilla, and food color. Measure flour and
blend with salt. Add flour and salt to rest of ingredients -- if too
dry, add 1-2 tablespoons cream. Wrap dough around chocolate kiss. Bake 1 inch apart on ungreased baking sheet 12-15
minutes at 350°. Cool. Dip tops in chosen icing and immediately dip tops in chopped nuts, coconut or colored sugar.

Icing:

1 cup powdered sugar
2 1/2 tablespoons cream
1 teaspoon vanilla
Red, green or yellow food color.

Mix together until smooth.

Chocolate Icing:

1 cup powdered sugar
1 square unsweetened chocolate
1 teaspoon vanilla
3 tablespoons cream

Melt chocolate; add cream and vanilla. Mix in powdered sugar
and beat until smooth.

SPLIT SECOND COOKIES

2 cups flour
2/3 cup sugar
Pinch of salt
1/2 teaspoon baking powder
3/4 cup butter, softened
1 egg
1 teaspoon vanilla
Red jelly or jam

Sift together flour, sugar, salt and baking powder. Cut in butter, unbeaten egg and vanilla. Form into dough. Place on lightly floured board. Divide into 4 parts. Shape into rolls 13 inches long, 3/4 inch thick. Put on ungreased cookie sheets, 4 inches apart and 3 inches from edge. Make a depression with handle of knife about 1/3 inch deep lengthwise and down the center of each. Fill with red jelly or jam (about 1/4 cup in all). Bake at 350°, 15-20 minutes, until golden brown. While warm, slice diagonally. Makes about 4 dozen.

CHOCOLATE-CHERRY THUMBPRINTS

3/4 cup sugar
2/3 cup margarine or butter, softened
2 eggs
1 teaspoon vanilla
1 12-ounce package semisweet chocolate chips, divided
2 cups oats, quick or old fashioned
1 1/2 cups all-purpose flour
1 teaspoon baking powder
1/4 teaspoon salt, optional
2 10-ounce jars maraschino cherries, drained, patted dry

Heat oven to 350°. Beat sugar, margarine, eggs and vanilla until smooth. Add 1 cup chips, melted; mix well. Stir in oats, flour, baking powder and salt; mix well. Cover; chill dough 1 hour. Shape dough into 1-inch balls. Place 2 inches apart on ungreased cookie sheet. Press deep centers with thumb. Place maraschino cherry into each center. Bake 10 to 12 minutes or until set. Remove to wire rack; cool completely. Drizzle cookies with remaining 1 cup chocolate chips, melted. Makes about 4 dozen.

PIZZELLES

6 eggs
3 1/2 cups flour (approximate)
1 1/2 cups sugar
1 cup margarine, melted
4 teaspoons baking powder
2 tablespoons vanilla or anise extract

Beat eggs, adding sugar gradually. Beat until smooth and thick. Add cooled, melted margarine and flavoring. Add flour and baking powder (sifted together) to egg mixture. Dough will be very sticky. Drop by rounded spoonful onto center of preheated pizzelle iron, close iron. Bake approximately 30 to 45 seconds or until pizzelle is lightly golden brown. Cool on wire rack. Store in airtight container. Serve plain or dusted with powdered sugar.

Chocolate Pizzelles:

1/2 cup cocoa
1/2 cup sugar
1/2 teaspoon baking powder

Add the above ingredients to plain pizzelle recipe. Sift with other dry ingredients. Use only vanilla extract. Bake the same. Optional - you may also add 1 cup of very finely chopped pecans or hazelnuts to recipe.

CHOCOLATE MINT SNOW-TOP COOKIES

1 1/2 cups flour
1 1/2 teaspoons baking powder
1/4 teaspoon salt
1 10-ounce package mint chocolate chips
6 tablespoons butter
1 cup sugar
1 1/2 teaspoons vanilla
2 eggs
Powdered sugar

Beat butter, sugar and eggs until creamy. Melt 1 cup mint chocolate chips. Add vanilla to melted chocolate and stir into sugar mixture. Gradually beat in flour, baking powder and salt. Stir in 1/2 cup mint chocolate chips. Wrap in plastic wrap and freeze. Shape dough in 1-inch balls; coat with powdered sugar. Place on ungreased cookie sheets. Bake at 350° for 10-15 minutes. Let stand 5 minutes before removing from cookie sheets.

NEAPOLITAN COOKIES

2 1/2 cups all-purpose flour
1 1/2 teaspoons baking powder
1/2 teaspoon salt
1 cup margarine or butter
1 1/2 cups sugar
1 egg
1 teaspoon vanilla
1/2 teaspoon almond extract
5 drops red food coloring
1/2 cup walnuts, finely chopped
1 square unsweetened chocolate, melted and cooled to
    room temperature

In a small mixing bowl, stir together flour, baking powder and salt; set aside. In a medium mixing bowl beat margarine or butter with an electric mixer on medium speed for 30 seconds. Add sugar and beat until fluffy. Add egg and vanilla; beat just until combined. Slowly add the flour mixture, beating on medium speed about 3 minutes or until combined.

Line a 9x5x3-inch loaf pan with waxed paper, allowing the ends of the paper to hang over the sides of the pan; set aside. Divide the dough into 3 portions. To one portion of the dough, stir in almond extract and red food coloring; pat onto the bottom of the pan. To another third of the dough, stir in chopped nuts; pat evenly over pink dough in pan. To the remaining dough, stir in melted chocolate; pat evenly over nut dough. Cover and chill at least 4 hours or until dough is firm enough to slice.

Lift the waxed paper to remove the chilled dough from the pan; remove the waxed paper. Cut the dough in half lengthwise, then slice each half crosswise into 1/8-1/4-inch thick slices. Arrange the slices about 1 inch apart on an ungreased cookie sheet.

Bake at 350° for 10-12 minutes or until edges are firm and light brown. Cool on cookie sheets for 1 minute. Transfer cookies to wire rack to cool completely. Makes 72 to 84 cookies.

HAZELNUT SPIRALS

Dough:

> 1 1/4 cups flour
> 1/3 cup sugar
> 1/4 teaspoon baking powder
> 1/8 teaspoon salt
> 10 tablespoons cold butter, cut into 10 pieces
> Yolk of 1 egg
> 1 teaspoon vanilla
> 1 tablespoon butter, softened

Combine all ingredients. Roll on lightly floured surface 18x6-inch or 2 9x6-inch pieces. Spread with 1 tablespoon butter. Set aside while preparing filling.

Filling:

> 3/4 cup hazelnuts, toasted and ground
> 1/4 cup sugar
> 1/4 teaspoon allspice
> 1/8 teaspoon nutmeg

Combine all ingredients. Press nut mixture into dough, leaving 1/2 inch at one end of dough. Roll up jelly roll fashion; pinch to seal; wrap in waxed paper and chill at least 1 hour. Slice 3/8 inch and place 1 inch apart on ungreased cookie sheets. Bake at 350° for 13 minutes. Makes 4 dozen cookies.

CHOCO-CARAMEL DELIGHTS

2/3 cup sugar
1/2 cup butter or margarine, softened
1 egg, separated
2 tablespoons milk
1 teaspoon vanilla
1 cup all-purpose flour
1/3 cup cocoa
1/4 teaspoon salt
1 cup pecans, finely chopped
Caramel filling
1/2 cup semisweet chocolate chips or chocolate chunks
1 teaspoon shortening

In small mixing bowl, beat sugar, butter, egg yolk, milk and vanilla until blended. Stir together flour, cocoa and salt; blend into butter mixture. Chill dough at least 1 hour or until firm enough to handle.

Preheat oven to 350°. Lightly grease cookie sheets. Beat egg white slightly. Shape dough into 1-inch balls. Dip each ball into egg whites; roll in pecans to coat. Place 1-inch apart on prepared cookie sheet. Press thumb gently in center of each ball. Bake at 350° for 10-12 minutes or until set. While cookies bake, prepare caramel filling. Press center of each cookie again with thumb to make indentation. Immediately spoon about 1/2 caramel filling into center of each cookie. Carefully remove to wire racks to cool completely.

In small microwave-safe bowl, combine chocolate chips and shortening. Microwave on high for 1 minute or until softened; stir. Allow to stand several minutes to finish melting; stir until smooth. Place waxed paper under wire racks with cookies. Drizzle chocolate mixture over top of cookies.

Caramel filling:
14 unwrapped light caramels
3 tablespoons whipping cream

Cook over low heat, stirring frequently, until caramels are melted and mixture is smooth.

ORANGE SLICES

1 cup butter, softened
1/2 cup powdered sugar
2 cups all-purpose flour
1/4 teaspoon baking powder
1/4 teaspoon salt
1 tablespoon orange peel, grated
1 tablespoon Grand Marnier
Orange food color
Orange gumdrops, finely chopped

Cream butter and sugar. Add dry ingredients. Add peel, liqueur and color. Wrap dough in plastic wrap and refrigerate 1 1/2 to 2 hours. Preheat oven to 350°. Work with 1/4 dough at a time. Keep remainder refrigerated. Roll dough out to 1/2-inch thickness. Cut out 3-inch rounds; cut in half. Score to resemble orange sections; decorate with orange gumdrops. Place on ungreased cookie sheets about 1-inch apart. Bake about 15 minutes at 350° only until lightly browned. When cool, sprinkle with powdered sugar. Makes 3-4 dozen.

MOLASSES SPICE SPRITZ

1/2 cup shortening
1/2 cup sugar
1 egg
1/4 tablespoon baking soda
1/4 cup molasses
2 cups flour
1/4 tablespoon salt
1/4 tablespoon allspice
1/4 tablespoon cloves
1/4 tablespoon mace
1/2 tablespoon cinnamon
1/2 teaspoon ginger

Cream shortening. Add sugar gradually. Add egg. Mix soda with molasses and add to creamed mixture. Gradually add flour sifted with salt and spices. Fill cookie press. Form on ungreased cookie sheets. Bake at 375° for 10 minutes. Remove cookies from sheets at once.

CASHEW CRISPS

2 cups all-purpose flour
3/4 cup butter, softened
3/4 cup sugar
1 1/2 teaspoons vanilla
1/4 teaspoon salt
4 ounces cashews
6-ounce package chocolate chips

Preheat oven to 350°. Into large bowl, measure flour, butter, sugar, vanilla and salt. Using hands, blend all ingredients until well mixed. Chop cashews; place on waxed paper. Roll level tablespoonfuls of dough into balls. Press one side of each ball into chopped nuts. Place flattened balls, nut-side up, on ungreased cookie sheet, about 2 inches apart. Bake cookies about 15 minutes or until lightly browned. Remove cookies to wire rack to cool. Then drizzle with melted chocolate chips (use double-boiler or microwave to melt). Makes 2 dozen.

THREE-IN-ONE COOKIES

Use this basic dough to make three kinds of cookies.

3/4 cup shortening
3/4 cup margarine or butter
4 1/2 cups all-purpose flour
1 1/2 teaspoons vanilla
1/4 teaspoon baking soda
1 1/2 cups sugar
1 egg
3 tablespoons milk
1 egg yolk
1/4 teaspoon salt

In large mixing bowl beat shortening and margarine or butter with an electric mixer on medium to high speed until softened. Add about half of the flour, all of the sugar, egg, milk, egg yolk, vanilla, baking soda and salt. Beat until thoroughly combined, scraping sides of bowl occasionally. Beat or stir in remaining flour. Divide dough into thirds.

Basic Frosting for Three-in-One Cookies

1/2 cup margarine or butter
4 cups sifted powdered sugar
3 tablespoons milk
1/2 teaspoon vanilla

In a small mixing bowl beat margarine or butter with an electric mixer on medium to high speed until softened. Gradually add 2 cups of the powdered sugar, beating until combined. Beat in milk and vanilla. Gradually beat in remaining powdered sugar until smooth. Divide frosting in half; use one-half to frost Choco-Mint Thumbprints and the other half to frost the Lemon Almond Tea Cookies.

With first third of basic dough make:

CHOCO-MINT THUMBPRINTS

1/3 of basic dough
2 squares semisweet chocolate, melted and cooled
2 teaspoons milk
1/2 recipe basic frosting
1 teaspoon milk
1/4 teaspoon peppermint extract
Few drops of green food coloring, optional
1/4 cup candy cane or peppermint candies, chopped

In medium bowl combine the cookie dough, chocolate and 2
teaspoons milk. Using a wooden spoon, mix until thoroughly
combined. Shape dough into an 8-inch roll. Wrap in waxed
paper or clear plastic wrap. Chill for at least 1-2 hours (or
freeze for same time if dough was made with corn oil margarine).

Cut dough into 3/4-inch slices. Cut each slice into
quarters. Shape each quarter into a ball. Place 2 inches apart
on an ungreased cookie sheet. Press down in the center of
each with your thumb. Bake cookies at 375° for 8-10 minutes
or until tops look dry. Transfer cookies to a wire rack to cool
completely.

Meanwhile, combine frosting, 1 teaspoon milk, peppermint extract and food coloring, if desired. Mix thoroughly.
Spoon a scant teaspoon of the filling into the center of each
cookie. Sprinkle each cookie with some of the chopped candy.
Makes about 48 cookies.

With second third of basic dough make:

LEMON ALMOND TEA COOKIES

1/3 of basic dough
2 teaspoons grated lemon peel
1 teaspoon almond extract.

To basic dough add lemon peel and almond extract. Shape
into 8-inch roll and chill or freeze 1-2 hours. Remove and cut
dough into 1/4-inch slices. Place 2-inches apart on ungreased
cookie sheet. Bake 375° for 8-10 minutes until bottoms are
lightly browned. Cool and frost.

To one-third of basic frosting recipe add 1 teaspoon
lemon juice. Mix well. Frost cookies and immediately top with
a few sliced almonds. Makes about 48 cookies.

With last third of basic dough make:

CHERRY PISTACHIO ROUNDS

1/3 basic dough
3/4 cup maraschino cherries, drained and finely
chopped
Red food coloring, if desired.
1/2 cup Pistachio nuts, finely chopped

Mix cherries and food coloring into basic dough. Shape into
10-inch roll. Roll in nuts (can use walnuts or pecans). Wrap in
plastic wrap and chill at least four hours (freeze for the same
time if corn oil margarine is used).

Remove from refrigerator. Cut dough in 1/4-inch thick
slices. Place 2 inches apart on ungreased cookie sheets. Bake
at 375° for about 10 minutes or until edges are firm and bottom light brown.

Add 1 teaspoon maraschino cherry juice to basic frosting. Mix together. Frost cookies and garnish with a few
chopped maraschino cherries. Makes 36 cookies.

116

CRANBERRY-HAZELNUT PHYLLO BASKETS

Phyllo Baskets:
    8 phyllo pastry sheets
    2 1/2 sticks unsalted butter, melted
    6 tablespoons dry breadcrumbs, finely ground

Place 1 phyllo sheet on work surface. (Cover remaining sheets with damp towel to prevent drying). Brush with 2 tablespoons melted butter. Sprinkle with 1 tablespoon breadcrumbs. Repeat with 3 more sheets; do not sprinkle fourth sheet with breadcrumbs. Repeat entire process 1 more time for total of 2 stacks of 4 sheets each. Mark off twenty 3-inch squares on each stack using a ruler. Cut into squares using scissors or pizza cutter. Preheat oven to 350°. Brush 40 miniature muffin cups with remaining butter. Press 1 stacked phyllo square into each muffin cup, forming basket. Bake until lightly browned, 10-12 minutes. Transfer baskets to rack; cool to room temperature (Can be prepared 2 weeks ahead. Store at room temperature).

Cranberry topping:
    1 12-ounce package cranberries
    1 1/2 cups sugar
    6 tablespoons water
Cook cranberries, sugar and water in heavy medium saucepan over low heat until sugar dissolves, swirling pan occasionally. Increase heat and bring to boil. Reduce heat and cook until berries pop, about 10 minutes. Refrigerate until cool. (Can be prepared 1 week ahead.)

Filling:
    10 ounce cream cheese, room temperature
    8 1/2 tablespoons powdered sugar
    1 1/4 tablespoons lemon peel
    2 1/2 teaspoons fresh lemon juice
    1/3 cup toasted, husked hazelnuts, coarsely chopped
Blend cream cheese and sugar with electric mixer until smooth and creamy. Stir in peel and juice.

To assemble: Divide cream cheese filling among phyllo baskets. Spoon 1 teaspoon cranberry topping over filling. Sprinkle with hazelnuts. (Can be prepared 4 hours ahead and refrigerate. Serve at room temperature).

117

FROSTED EGGNOG LOGS

3 cups flour
1 teaspoon ground nutmeg
1 cup butter or margarine
3/4 cup sugar
1 egg
2 teaspoons vanilla
1-2 teaspoons rum flavoring
Rum Frosting

In mixing bowl stir together the flour and nutmeg. In a large mixing bowl or food processor bowl beat butter until softened. Add sugar and beat until fluffy. Beat in the egg, vanilla and rum flavoring. Add dry ingredients and beat well. Shape dough into long, pencil-like rolls. Cut into 3-inch long logs. Arrange on ungreased cookie sheets. Bake at 350° for 12-15 minutes or until golden brown. Remove and cool.

Meanwhile prepare rum frosting. Frost tops of cooled logs; mark frosting lengthwise with lines of a fork to resemble bark. Sprinkle with additional nutmeg.

Rum Frosting:

4 ounces cream cheese
3 tablespoons butter or margarine
1 1/2 cups powdered sugar
1 teaspoon rum flavoring
1/2 teaspoon vanilla

Beat cream cheese and butter until well blended. Add flavorings and gradually beat in powdered sugar. If too stiff to spread add a few drops of milk.

ALMOND COOKIES

1 cup shortening
1 cup margarine
2 cups sugar
1 teaspoon vanilla
1/2 teaspoon almond flavoring or extract
3 1/2 cups flour
1 teaspoon soda
1 cup sliced almonds
1 cup coconut

Cream shortening, margarine and sugar together. Add flavorings. Mix in flour and soda. Add almonds and coconut. Chill well. Roll into small balls. Press with bottom of glass dipped in sugar. Bake at 350° for 10-12 minutes. Makes 9-10 dozen.

SNOWBALLS

Filling:

1 6-ounce package milk chocolate morsels
1/4 cup powdered sugar, sifted
1/3 cup almonds, finely chopped

Melt chocolate. Stir in powdered sugar and nuts. Chill until firm enough to handle. Shape into 3/4-inch balls.

Cookie dough:

3 cups flour
1 1/4 cups unsalted margarine
2 teaspoons vanilla
1/2-2/3 cups powdered sugar

Beat flour, margarine and vanilla until fluffy and smooth. Turn dough onto lightly floured surface and shape into 11-inch log. Cut into 1/4-inch slices. Shape cookie dough around chocolate ball and shape into a round ball. Place 1-inch apart on ungreased cookie sheets. Bake at 400° for 10 minutes or until lightly browned. Cool 5 minutes and roll in powdered sugar. Makes 4 dozen.

NUT CUPS

     1 stick butter
     1 cup flour
     1 3-ounce package cream cheese

Make sure all dough ingredients are at room temperature. Mix all ingredients together and divide evenly into 2 balls. Roll one ball into a thick rope. Cut the rope into 12 equal pieces. Repeat process with second ball. Place one piece of dough into a miniature (1 3/4-inch) metal baking tin (not paper cups). Repeat until all dough is used. Flatten dough on the bottom of each tin being careful not to make too thin. Set aside and make filling.

Filling:
     1 egg, beaten
     1/2 stick butter
     1 cup pecans, crushed
     3/4 cup brown sugar
     1 teaspoon vanilla
     Dash of salt

Combine all ingredients. Pour over each cookie, filling each tin to the top. Bake at 350° for 20-30 minutes. Dust with powdered sugar.

NUT-EDGED BUTTER SLICES

1 1/2 cups all-purpose flour, sifted
2 teaspoons baking powder
1/2 teaspoon salt
1/2 cup butter
2/3 cup sugar
1 egg yolk
2 tablespoons light cream
1 teaspoon vanilla
1/2 cup toasted almonds, finely chopped
3 tablespoons sugar
1 egg white, slightly beaten

Sift together flour, baking powder and salt. Cream butter and 2/3 cup sugar; add egg yolk, cream and vanilla. Beat well. Add flour mixture gradually, beating well. Shape dough on waxed paper into 12x1 1/2-inch roll. Chill 1 hour.

Combine almonds and 3 tablespoons sugar. Brush chilled dough with egg white and roll in almond mixture, pressing nuts in firmly. Cut 1/4-inch slices. Place on lightly greased cookie sheet. Bake at 400° for 7-10 minutes. Makes about 4 dozen cookies.

SNOW-TOPPED THUMBPRINTS

2/3 cup maple syrup
1/2 cup margarine, softened
1 3-ounce package cream cheese, softened
1 egg
2 cups all-purpose flour
1 1/3 cups nuts, chopped
1 teaspoon baking powder
1/4 teaspoon salt
1/3 cup fruit preserves

Heat oven to 350°. Beat first 4 ingredients until smooth. Add dry ingredients; mix well. Chill 10 minutes. Roll into 1-inch balls; place on ungreased cookie sheets. Press center of each with thumb. Fill with your favorite preserves. Bake 9-11 minutes or until edges are golden. Cool completely. Sprinkle with powdered sugar, if desired. Store in loosely covered container.

SHORTBREAD STARS

2 cups butter, softened
1 cup sugar
5 cups flour
1 tablespoon almond flavoring
2 squares semisweet chocolate, melted
1/2 cup pistachio nuts, chopped

Cream butter and sugar. Gradually add flour and almond flavoring. Chill dough. Roll out dough to 1/3-1/2 inch thick. Cut cookies with star-shaped cutter. Place on ungreased baking sheet and bake 20-25 minutes at 300°. (Tops do not brown, nor do cookies change shape during baking.) When cool, drizzle with melted semisweet chocolate and sprinkle with chopped pistachio nuts while chocolate is still warm Makes about 4 dozen cookies.

CHERRY WINKIES

1/3 cup shortening
1/2 cup sugar
1 egg, well beaten
1 teaspoon lemon rind, grated
1 teaspoon vanilla
1 1/2 tablespoons maraschino cherry juice
1 cup flour
1/4 teaspoon salt
1/4 teaspoon soda
1/2 teaspoon baking powder
1/2 cup raisins, chopped, optional
1/2 cup nuts, chopped
1 cup corn flakes, crushed
24 maraschino cherries

Cream shortening and sugar thoroughly. Add egg, lemon rind, vanilla and juice. Beat well. Sift together flour, salt, soda and baking powder. Add to other mixture. Beat in raisins and nuts. Drop by teaspoonfuls into crushed flakes and roll into balls. Place on greased cookie sheets and top with cherry. Bake at 400° for 10 minutes or until browned. Makes 24.

MOLASSES SUGAR COOKIES

3/4 cup margarine, softened
1 cup sugar
1/4 cup molasses
1 egg
2 teaspoons soda
2 cups flour
1/2 teaspoon cloves
1/2 teaspoon ginger
1/2 teaspoon cinnamon
1/2 teaspoon salt

Mix together. Roll into small balls and roll in sugar. Bake at 375° for 8-10 minutes.

OATMEAL TOFFEE COOKIES

1 1/2 cups old-fashioned oats, uncooked
3/4 cup all-purpose flour
3/4 cup sugar
1/3 cup brown sugar
6 tablespoons butter or margarine, softened
1 teaspoon vanilla extract
1/2 teaspoon baking soda
1/2 teaspoon baking powder
1/4 teaspoon salt
1 egg
5 small chocolate covered toffee bars, cut into 1/2-inch
    pieces

Into large bowl measure all ingredients except toffee bars. Mix on low speed until well blended. With spoon, stir in toffee bar pieces. Preheat oven to 350°. Shape 1 heaping tablespoonful of dough one at a time into a ball, arranging about 2 inches apart on slightly greased baking sheet. Flatten slightly. Bake about 12 minutes. Store cookies in tightly covered container. Makes about 2 1/2 dozen cookies.

KOLACHKY COOKIES

1 pound butter or margarine
1 cup sugar
2 eggs
4 cups flour, sifted
1 can apricot or prune filling

Cream together butter and sugar. Add eggs and flour and mix well. Divide dough into 4 equal parts. Put in waxed paper and roll into logs. Store over night in refrigerator or at least 2 hours. Take dough out of waxed paper and slice thin. Spoon apricot or prune filling onto every cookie. DO NOT GREASE PAN. Bake at 375° for 10-12 minutes. Cool. Roll in powdered sugar.

LITTLE DIPPERS

1/2 cup butter, softened
1/2 cup sugar
1 large egg
2 cups all-purpose flour
1 teaspoon baking powder
1 tablespoon orange peel, grated
1 teaspoon orange extract
4 1-ounce squares semisweet chocolate

In large bowl with electric mixer at medium speed, beat butter and sugar until light and fluffy; beat egg in well. At low speed beat in flour and baking powder to blend well. Beat in orange peel and orange extract. Flatten dough to disk shape. Wrap in plastic and refrigerate at least 1 hour until firm.

Heat oven to 375°. Work with half the dough at a time; keep remainder refrigerated. Using cookie press fitted with large star tip, pipe into 3-inch lengths onto ungreased cookie sheets, spacing about 1 inch apart. Bake 10 minutes or until firm to touch and edges are lightly browned. Cool on racks. Dip one end of each cooled cookie into melted semisweet chocolate to coat halfway. Decorate with chopped mixed candied fruits. Makes about 4 dozen.

CREAM CHEESE SUGAR COOKIES

1 cup butter or margarine, room temperature
1 3-ounce package cream cheese, room temperature
3/4 cup sugar
1 egg
Pinch of salt
2 teaspoons vanilla
1/2 teaspoon almond extract, optional
3 cups all-purpose flour
Red and green sugar crystals, optional

Beat together first seven ingredients until light and fluffy. Add flour gradually until well blended. Divide dough into 2 equal portions. Wrap and refrigerate for several hours or overnight. Prior to baking allow dough to stand at room temperature until soft enough to roll easily. Preheat oven to 375°. On floured surface, roll dough to 1/4-inch thick. Cut into desired shapes. Sprinkle with colored sugar crystals, if desired. Makes about 45 3-inch cookies.

QUICK AND EASY MARBLE COOKIES

1 6-ounce package chocolate chips
1 marble cake mix
1 egg
1/3 cup vegetable oil
4 tablespoons water

Mix yellow part of cake mix, egg, 3 tablespoons water and oil. Combine the chocolate part of the cake mix and 1 tablespoon water; mix well and add to 1/4 of the yellow cake mixture. To the remaining part of the yellow mix, add the chocolate chips. To form cookies, take 1 teaspoonful of yellow dough and a pinch of chocolate dough on either side of the yellow dough and form into a ball. Place on ungreased cookie sheet and flatten slightly. Bake at 350° for 6-8 minutes.

PEANUT BUTTER FINGERS

1 package active dry yeast
2 tablespoons warm water (105°-115°)
1/2 cup sugar
1/2 cup brown sugar, packed
1 egg
1/2 cup creamy or chunky peanut butter
1/4 cup butter or margarine, softened
1/4 cup shortening
1 1/2 cups all-purpose flour
3/4 teaspoon baking soda
1/4 teaspoon salt

Dissolve yeast in warm water in large bowl. Mix in sugars, egg, peanut butter, margarine and shortening until smooth. Stir in flour, baking soda and salt. Cover and refrigerate 30 minutes. Heat oven to 375°. Shape dough by teaspoonfuls into 2 1/2-inch fingers on ungreased cookie sheet. Bake until light brown, about 8 minutes. Cool. Dip one end of each cookie into cocoa glaze. Makes about 6 dozen cookies.

Cocoa glaze:

1 1/2 cups powdered sugar
1/4 cup cocoa
3 tablespoons milk
1 teaspoon vanilla

Mix sugar and cocoa in medium bowl. Stir in milk and vanilla until smooth. Stir in additional milk, 1/2 teaspoon at a time, until of desired consistency.

MACADAMIA SNOWBALLS

These bite-sized confections blend two intriguing flavors--
rum and crunchy macadamia nuts from the South Pacific.
They are great to make ahead and keep fresh in a pretty tin
throughout the Holidays--if they last that long!!

> 8 tablespoons unsalted butter at room temperature
> 1 cup all-purpose flour
> 4 tablespoons dark rum
> 1 teaspoon vanilla extract
> 1/4 teaspoon salt
> 1 1/4 cups macadamia nuts, finely chopped
> 1 cup powdered sugar

Cream the butter. Continue beating and gradually add the flour, rum, vanilla and salt. Mix well. Stir in chopped macadamia nuts, then beat on slow speed until nuts are mixed through evenly. Wrap dough in plastic wrap and refrigerate for 1 hour.

Preheat oven to 300°. Spray cookie sheets with vegetable cooking spray. Form balls by hand so they are 3/4 inches in diameter. Bake on middle rack of oven for 35 minutes. Remove from oven. Cool slightly and roll in powdered sugar. When completely cool, roll in sugar again to give a snowy appearance. Makes 32 snowballs.

CHERRY PECAN COOKIES

1 cup butter or margarine, softened
1 cup sifted powdered sugar
1 egg
2 1/2 cups all-purpose flour
1/4 teaspoon cream of tartar
1 cup candied cherries, halved
1/2 cup pecans, finely chopped

Cream butter. Gradually add sugar, beating until light and fluffy. Add egg and beat well. Combine flour and cream of tartar. Add to creamed mixture and mix well. Stir in cherries and pecans. Shape dough into two 10x2-inch rolls. Wrap in aluminum foil and freeze until firm. Cut into 1/4-inch slices. Place on ungreased cookie sheets. Bake at 375° for 10-12 minutes (light tan on edges). Makes 6 1/2 dozen.

OLD TYME LEMON CRISPS

3/4 cup butter or margarine, softened
1 3-ounce package cream cheese, softened
3/4 cup sugar
2 tablespoons grated lemon peel
1 tablespoon lemon juice, freshly squeezed
2 cups all-purpose flour
1/4 teaspoon salt.

In large bowl with electric mixer at medium speed, beat butter, cream cheese, sugar, lemon peel and lemon juice until light and fluffy. With mixer at low speed beat in flour and salt to blend well. Flatten dough to disc shape and refrigerate 30 minutes. Work with 1/4 of dough at a time. Keep remainder refrigerated. Heat oven to 350°. Roll out to 1/4-inch thickness, cut into 2-inch rounds. Use coarse end of meat mallet or fork to make design. Sprinkle with yellow sugar crystals. Bake 10-12 minutes. Makes about 3 dozen.

CHRISTMAS SNICKERDOODLES

1 cup butter
1 1/2 cups sugar
2 eggs
2 teaspoons vanilla
2 3/4 cups flour
1 tablespoon baking powder

Melt butter in saucepan or microwave. Remove from heat. Stir in sugar and vanilla until blended. Let cool slightly. Add eggs. Beat with spoon until blended. Add flour and baking powder until blended. Chill 1-3 hours or freeze for 15 minutes. Roll into 1-inch balls and roll in *sprinkle mixture. Bake on ungreased cookie sheet for 10 minutes at 350°. Makes 5 dozen.

*Sprinkle mixture:

1/4 cup sugar
2 teaspoons cinnamon
Red and/or green sprinkles

MILLION DOLLAR CHOCOLATE BAR COOKIES

This recipe can be halved or quartered.

2 cups butter
2 cups sugar
2 cups brown sugar
4 eggs
2 teaspoons vanilla
4 cups flour
2 teaspoons baking soda
5 cups blended oats*
1 teaspoon salt
2 teaspoons baking powder
24-ounce package chocolate chips
1 8-ounce chocolate bar, grated
3 cups nuts, chopped

*Blender oats: Measure and blend in a blender to a fine powder.

Cream butter and both sugars. Add eggs and vanilla. Mix together with flour, oats, salt, baking powder and baking soda. Add chips, candy and nuts. Roll into balls and place 2 inches apart on a cookie sheet. Bake for 6 minutes at 375°. Makes 112 cookies.

CELEBRITY SUGAR COOKIES

2 cups sugar
1 cup shortening
2-3 eggs
Pinch of salt
1 teaspoon vanilla
1 teaspoon lemon extract
1/2 cup milk
1 teaspoon baking soda
1 teaspoon baking powder
4 cups flour

Mix all ingredients together. Roll into small balls. Bake 8-10 minutes at 350°. Frost with canned sour cream frosting and top with confetti sprinkles.

POPPY SEED-NUT SLICES

1 cup butter, softened
1 cup plus 2 tablespoons sugar
1 large egg
1 teaspoon vanilla
1/2 teaspoon cinnamon
1 1/2 cups almonds, finely chopped
1/2 cup poppy seeds
2 cups flour
1/4 teaspoon salt

Beat butter and sugar in mixer bowl until light and fluffy. Add egg, vanilla and cinnamon. Beat 2-3 minutes. Add nuts and poppy seeds. Beat 1 minute more. Gradually stir in flour and salt. Refrigerate until dough is firm (about 2 hours). Shape into 2 rolls about 2 inches in diameter. Roll in 1 tablespoon sugar. Wrap in waxed paper and refrigerate 3 hours. Slice dough 1/4- inch thick. Place on ungreased baking sheets. Bake at 325° for 20 minutes or until edges begin to brown. Makes 6 dozen.

COCOA PEANUT-BUTTER KISSES

These cookies are best the day they are baked, but leftovers can be frozen.

> 1 cup all-purpose flour
> 1/4 cup unsweetened cocoa powder
> 1 teaspoon baking soda
> 1/2 cup butter or margarine, at room temperature
> 3/4 cup creamy peanut butter
> 1/3 cup plus 1/4 cup granulated sugar
> 1/3 cup light brown sugar, packed
> 1 large egg
> 1 tablespoon milk
> 1 teaspoon vanilla extract
> 48 milk chocolate kisses

Heat oven to 375°. Mix flour, cocoa and baking soda. Beat butter and peanut butter in a large bowl with electric mixer until creamy. Add 1/3 cup sugar and the brown sugar; beat until fluffy. Beat in egg, milk and vanilla until well blended. With mixer on low speed gradually beat in flour mixture just until blended. Shape heaping teaspoonfuls into balls. Roll in remaining 1/4 cup sugar to coat. Place 1 1/2 inches apart on ungreased cookie sheets. Bake 10-12 minutes until firm. Immediately place a chocolate kiss on each cookie, pressing down so that cookie cracks about the edge. Remove to racks to cool completely. Makes 48 cookies.

FANCY WALNUT BROWNIES

Brownies:

> 1 package Chocolate Lovers' Walnut Brownie Mix
> 1 egg
> 1/3 cup water
> 1/3 cup oil

Glaze:

> 4 1/2 cups powdered sugar
> 1/2 cup milk or water
> 24 walnut halves, for garnish

Chocolate Drizzle:

> 1/3 cup semisweet chocolate chips
> 1 tablespoon shortening

Preheat oven to 350°. Place 24 (2-inch) foil liners on baking sheets. Combine brownie mix, egg, water and oil in large bowl. Stir with spoon until well blended, about 50 strokes. Stir in contents of walnut packet from Mix. Fill each foil liner with 2 generous tablespoons batter. Bake at 350° for 20 to 25 minutes or until set. Cool completely. Remove liners. Turn brownies upside down on cooling racks.

Glaze: Combine powdered sugar and milk in medium bowl. Blend until smooth. Spoon glaze over each brownie to completely cover. Top immediately with walnut half. Allow glaze to set.

Chocolate drizzle: Place chocolate chips and shortening in small resealable plastic bag; seal. Place bag in bowl of hot water for several minutes. Dry with paper towel. Knead until blended chocolate is smooth. Snip pinpoint hole in corner of bag. Drizzle chocolate over brownies. Allow chocolate drizzle to set before storing in single layer in airtight containers.

LEMON BLOSSOMS

1 1/4 cups all-purpose flour
1/2 teaspoon baking powder
1/4 teaspoon salt
3 tablespoons unsalted butter
3 tablespoons margarine
1/2 cup sugar
1 egg
1/2 teaspoon lemon juice

Glaze:

1-2 tablespoons lemon juice
1 cup powdered sugar

Stir together flour, baking powder and salt in medium bowl.
Set aside. Beat butter, margarine, sugar, egg and lemon juice
in bowl until well blended. Stir in flour mixture. Refrigerate for
1 hour. Use cookie gun with blossom tip. Thinly coat a cookie
sheet with cooking spray. Press cookies onto sheet and bake
10-12 minutes at 350°. When cool, frost with glaze and sprinkle with chopped pistachio nuts. Makes approximately
2 1/2 dozen.

Low Fat Cookies

LOW FAT COOKIES INDEX

LOW FAT PUMPKIN SPICE COOKIES

1 cup applesauce
1 package dry butter buds mix (not diluted)
1 cup sugar
1 egg substitute
1 cup canned pumpkin
2 cups flour
1 teaspoon baking soda
1 teaspoon cinnamon
1/4 teaspoon ginger
1/4 teaspoon ground cloves
1/2 teaspoon salt
1 cup grape-nuts cereal

Topping:

3 tablespoons sugar
1 teaspoon cinnamon

Preheat oven to 375°. Spray cookie sheets with a non-fat cooking spray. In a large bowl blend applesauce, dry butter buds, sugar, egg substitute and pumpkin. Mix together dry ingredients and mix with wet mixture. Add cereal. Chill dough 30 minutes. Drop by teaspoons onto cookie sheets. Bake 10-12 minutes. Sprinkle warm cookies with cinnamon and sugar mixture. Makes 7 dozen cookies.

Hint: To make your own egg substitute:

1 tablespoon nonfat dry milk powder
2 large egg whites
4 drops yellow food color

Beat dry milk powder and egg whites with fork until smooth. Add food color. Beat until well blended. Equivalent to 1 large egg.

LUSCIOUS AND LOW-FAT BUTTER-NUT SUGAR COOKIES

1 cup plus 2 tablespoons brown sugar, firmly packed
3 ounces Neufchatel cheese (about 1/3 cup)
1/4 cup plus 2 tablespoons margarine, softened
2 tablespoons skim milk
1/2 teaspoon vanilla
1/2 teaspoon butter flavoring
1/2 teaspoon almond extract
1 egg
3 cups all-purpose flour
1 1/2 teaspoons baking powder
1/2 teaspoon salt

Cream first 3 ingredients at medium speed of an electric mixer until light and fluffy. Add milk and next 2 ingredients, and beat well. Combine flour, baking powder, and salt. Add to creamed mixture, beating well. Divide dough into 4 equal portions. Working with one portion of dough at a time, roll out to 1/8-inch thickness on a well-floured surface; cover and refrigerate remaining dough. Cut dough with a 2-inch decorative cookie cutter; place cookies 1 inch apart on cookie sheets. Bake at 350° for 10 minutes; cool on wire racks. Repeat procedure with remaining dough.

Frosting:

1/2 cup powdered sugar, sifted
1 1/2 teaspoons water
Food coloring, optional

Combine powdered sugar, water, and food coloring, if desired; stir well. Spoon into a decorating bag fitted with a small round tip; pipe onto cookie. Makes 8 dozen cookies.

BROWNIES

1 cup flour
1 cup powdered sugar
1/4 cup plus 1/2 tablespoon unsweetened cocoa
    powder
3/4 teaspoon baking powder
1/4 cup semisweet chocolate chips
3 tablespoons margarine
1/2 cup brown sugar
2 tablespoons light corn syrup
1 tablespoon water
2 teaspoons vanilla
2 large egg whites

Preheat oven to 350°. Spray pan liberally with nonstick spray. Sift together first four ingredients; set aside. Melt chocolate and margarine in microwave, stirring until smooth. Stir in brown sugar, corn syrup, water and vanilla until well blended. Beat egg whites into chocolate mixture. Gently add dry ingredients to chocolate mixture just until well blended and smooth. Spread evenly in prepared pan. Bake on middle oven rack for 24-25 minutes, until center top is almost firm. Cool. Cut into 12 bars.

SOFT PEANUT BUTTER COOKIES

1/2 cup raisins
1/2 cup dates, chopped
1 ripe medium banana, mashed
1/3 cup creamy peanut butter
1/4 cup water
2 egg whites
1 teaspoon vanilla
1 cup oats
1/2 cup whole wheat flour
1 teaspoon baking soda

Combine raisins, dates, banana, peanut butter, water, egg
whites and vanilla in mixing bowl. Add oats, flour and soda.
Mix well. Drop by teaspoonfuls onto heavily sprayed baking
pan. Bake at 350° for 10 minutes.

FAT FREE CHEWY CHOCOLATE COOKIES

1 1/2 cups flour
1/2 cup sugar
1/2 cup unsweetened cocoa
1/2 teaspoon baking soda
1/2 teaspoon salt
1/2 cup light or dark corn syrup
3 egg whites

Combine flour, sugar, cocoa, baking soda and salt. Stir in egg
whites and syrup until blended. Dough will be thick and slightly
sticky. Drop by teaspoonfuls onto cookies sheets sprayed with
no-stick cooking spray. Bake at 350° for 7-9 minutes or until
set. Fingerprint will still remain when touched. Do not overbake. Makes 2 1/2 dozen.

OATMEAL RAISIN COOKIES

These cookies have a chewy, soft texture.

> 1/2 cup canola oil
> 1 cup brown sugar
> 4 egg whites
> 2 tablespoons low-fat milk
> 2 teaspoons vanilla
> 1 teaspoon cinnamon
> 1 teaspoon salt
> 1 teaspoon baking soda
> 1 1/2 cups oats
> 1 cup raisins
> 1 1/2 cups flour (can be mixed half white and
> half whole wheat)
> 1 cup nuts, chopped, optional

Preheat oven to 375°. Mix together the oil, sugar, egg whites, milk and vanilla. Beat well. Add soda, oats, cinnamon, salt and raisins. Mix well. Gently stir in the flour and nuts. Drop by rounded teaspoonfuls onto lightly sprayed baking sheet. Bake at 375° for 8-10 minutes or until firm.

Hint: Mixing equal portions of white and wheat flour gives cookies more texture.

CHOCOLATE COOKIES

1 cup flour
2/3 cup unsweetened cocoa
1/2 cup polyunsaturated margarine
1/2 cup sugar

Preheat oven to 350°. Spray cookie sheets with vegetable cooking spray. Sift together the flour and cocoa and set aside. Cream margarine and sugar until light and fluffy. Gradually blend in the flour mixture and mix until a dough is formed. Divide dough into small balls and place on cookie sheet. Dip a fork in hot water and flatten each cookie with tines. Bake 8-10 minutes. Remove from the cookie sheets while still hot, and place on racks to cool. Makes 48 cookies.

OATMEAL COOKIES

2 egg whites
1/2 teaspoon salt
2 cups sugar
2 cups oats
1/2 cup walnuts, chopped
1 teaspoon vanilla
2 tablespoons skim milk

Preheat oven to 350°. Spray cookie sheets with vegetable cooking spray. Drop dough from teaspoon about 1 inch apart onto cookie sheets. Bake at 350° for 12 minutes. Makes 48 cookies.

OLD-FASHIONED OATMEAL SPICE COOKIES

1 cup all-purpose flour
1/2 teaspoon baking powder
1/2 teaspoon salt
1/3 cup margarine
1/3 cup honey
1 teaspoon cinnamon
1/2 teaspoon ginger
1/4 teaspoon nutmeg
1 teaspoon vanilla
2 large egg whites
1/2 teaspoon lemon peel
1 cup quick-cooking oats
1/2 cup raisins

Preheat oven to 375°. Spray cookie sheets with vegetable cooking spray. Sift together flour, baking powder and salt. Set aside. Beat together margarine, honey, cinnamon, ginger, nutmeg and vanilla. Blend in egg whites and lemon peel. Add flour mixture, oats and raisins and mix well. Drop by teaspoonfuls onto cookies sheets 1 1/2 inches apart. Bake 8-10 minutes or until golden brown. Remove to racks and allow to cool. Makes 5 dozen cookies.

FORGOTTEN WALNUT KISSES

Easy, easy, easy! These will be the last thing you do at night and the first thing you tend to in the morning. Sure to be a hit!

> 3 egg whites
> Pinch of salt
> Pinch of cream of tartar
> 1 cup sugar
> 1 teaspoon vanilla
> 1 cup walnuts, finely chopped

Heat oven to 350°. Beat whites until frothy. Add salt and tartar. Keep beating, gradually adding sugar. Fold in vanilla and walnuts. Drop onto ungreased baking sheets. Turn oven off and leave cookies in oven several hours or overnight. Makes about 24 cookies.

SPICY APPLESAUCE COOKIES

1/2 cup polyunsaturated oil
1 cup brown sugar
2 egg whites
2 cups flour
1/2 teaspoon baking soda
1/2 teaspoon salt
1/2 teaspoon nutmeg
1/2 teaspoon cinnamon
1/2 teaspoon cloves
1/4 cup strong, cold coffee
1 cup applesauce
1/2 cup raisins, chopped
1/4 cup walnuts, coarsely chopped

Blend together oil and sugar. Add egg whites and beat until light and fluffy. Add coffee and applesauce. Sift together and add dry ingredients one cup at a time. Stir in raisins and walnuts. Drop by teaspoonfuls onto a sprayed cookie sheet. Bake at 400° for 9-12 minutes. Makes 48 cookies.

MASHED POTATO COOKIES

1 cup flour
1 teaspoon baking powder
1/2 teaspoon cinnamon
1/4 teaspoon cloves
1/4 teaspoon nutmeg
1/4 teaspoon salt
1/4 cup sugar
1/3 cup corn syrup
1/3 cup polyunsaturated oil
1/2 cup hot mashed potatoes, without seasonings
1/4 cup raisins
1/4 cup walnuts, chopped

Preheat oven to 375°. Spray cookie sheets. Sift together dry ingredients, except sugar and set aside. Blend together sugar, syrup, oil and potatoes. Add dry ingredients; mix well. Add raisins and walnuts. Mix well. Drop from teaspoon onto cookie sheets. Bake at 375° for 20 minutes. Makes 30 cookies.

CEREAL MACAROONS

Cereal replaces coconut to make this unusual mock cookie.

2 egg whites
Pinch of salt
Pinch of cream of tartar
2/3 cup sugar
1/2 teaspoon vanilla
1 cup walnuts, finely chopped
2 cups dry cereal (i.e. corn flakes, wheaties, bran flakes)

Beat egg whites until foamy. Add salt and tartar. Add sugar gradually, beating until stiff. Fold in vanilla, walnuts and cereal. Drop by spoonfuls onto sprayed baking sheets. Bake at 400° for 12 minutes or until delicately brown. Makes 36 cookies.

WHOLE WHEAT RAISIN COOKIES

2 tablespoons margarine
2 tablespoons nonfat yogurt
1 egg white, beaten until frothy
3 tablespoons dark brown sugar
1 teaspoon vanilla
1/2 teaspoon baking soda
1/2 cup unbleached flour
1/2 cup whole wheat flour
1/4 cup raisins, chopped

Preheat oven to 400°. Mix margarine, yogurt, egg white, sugar and vanilla in medium bowl using mixer. Sift together soda and flours. Stir in raisins. Add to the wet ingredients and combine until moistened. Spray cookie sheets with vegetable cooking spray. Form dough into small balls and place on cookie sheets. Flatten with the bottom of a glass. Bake at 400° for about 10 minutes. Let cookies cool on wire rack. Store in tightly covered tin. Makes 24 cookies.

DATE BARS

1 1/2 cups flour, sifted
1 teaspoon baking soda
1/4 teaspoon salt
1 1/4 cups oats
1 cup brown sugar
1/3 cup oil
2 tablespoons skim milk
1 package pitted dates, chopped
1/2 cup sugar
1 teaspoon flour
1 cup hot water
1 teaspoon vanilla

Cook the dates, sugar, flour and hot water until thick. Add vanilla. Cool. Sift together 1 1/2 cups flour, baking soda and salt. Add oats, sugar and oil. Add milk slowly and mix well. Pat half of mixture firmly into lightly sprayed 8-inch cake pan. When date mixture is cool, spread over crust mixture. Sprinkle remaining crust mixture evenly over the top and lightly pat down into date filling. Bake at 350° for 30 minutes. Cool and cut into 24 bars.

COOKIE EXCHANGE INDEX

NOTES:

NOTES:

NOTES:

Name _____

Address _____

City/State/Zip _____

Telephone (_____) _____

E-Mail _____

Please send best-selling cookbooks as indicated below:

	QUANTITY	PRICE	TAX (Colorado Residents Only)	TOTAL
COLORADO COOKIE COLLECTION	_____	$ 14.95	$ .45 per book	$_____
NOTHIN' BUT MUFFINS	_____	$ 12.95	$ .39 per book	$_____
101 WAYS TO MAKE RAMEN NOODLES	_____	$ 9.95	$ .30 per book	$_____
COOKIE EXCHANGE	_____	$ 12.95	$ .39 per book	$_____
QUICK CROCKERY COOKING	_____	$ 14.95	$ .45 per book	$_____
QUICK MEXICAN COOKING	_____	$ 14.95	$ .45 per book	$_____
QUICK SOUPS 'N SALADS	_____	$ 14.95	$ .45 per book	$_____

Shipping & Handling $2.00 for the first book & $1.00 for each additional book $_____

Please indicate payment method below   TOTAL ENCLOSED $_____

☐ Check   ☐ Money Order   ☐ MasterCard   ☐ Visa
Please make checks payable to: Please see reverse   Please see reverse

C & G Publishing, Inc.
P.O. Box 5199 • Greeley, CO 80634-0103 • (800) 925-3172

If using Visa or MasterCard, please fill in the following:

Name_____

Address_____

City/State/Zip_____

Telephone (_____)_____

Please charge this order to my ☐ Visa ☐ MasterCard

Account Number ⬚⬚⬚⬚⬚⬚⬚⬚⬚⬚⬚⬚⬚⬚⬚⬚⬚⬚

Expiration Date _____/_____
                 month   year

Customer Signature_____